MW00615989

INVESTMENT
ADVISOR
Marketing

INVESTMENT ADVISOR

Marketing

A Pathway to Growing Your Firm
and Building Your Brand

Scott Hanson *&* Pat McClain

with Sean Harvey

IRISH
CANON
PRESS

BERKELEY • CALIFORNIA

Investment Advisor Marketing:
A Pathway to Growing Your Firm and Building Your Brand

IRISH
CANON
PRESS

For sales, bulk discounts, or further information please contact:
Irish Canon Press, LLC
2625 Alcatraz Avenue Ste. #105
Berkeley, CA 94705
info@IrishCanonPress.com
www.IrishCanonPress.com

Cover and interior design by Williams Writing, Editing & Design

ISBN 978-0-9898754-0-0

Library of Congress Control Number 2013949318

IMPORTANT NOTE

The publisher, author, and editors, as well as the professionals quoted in the book, cannot be held responsible for any error, omission, or dated material. The author and publisher assume no responsibility for any outcome of applying the information in this book in a program or business or training setting.

This book is dedicated to all the team members
who make the Hanson McClain Group go.

A special "thank you" to
Sean Harvey for his assistance in helping us write
Investment Advisor Marketing:
A Pathway to Growing Your Firm
and Building Your Brand.
As the vice president of communications
for Hanson McClain Advisors,
Sean does writing, research, and marketing
for our firm, and he made
important creative contributions
toward the completion of this project.

CONTENTS

SECTION 2

Community Involvement

SECTION 3
Niche Marketing

SECTION 4
Assessments and Analytics

INTRODUCTION

Here's a question for you to answer: What types of things do you as an investment advisor need to do to grow your practice? Please consider that for a moment. What do investment advisors really need to do to increase their business?

Before we wrote a word of this book we compiled a list of the various topics we thought every advisor would want to know if they were just starting out, or if they were looking to improve their practices and expand their bottom lines. As we looked back on our combined four decades of experience, we had very little trouble coming up with a comprehensive list of "needs" and "musts." The fact is, we quickly had almost 100 items on the list, which started out highly specific, and included things like office setup, what coffee table books to place in the lobby, even stationery design, before we eventually expanded those to include office location, signage, continuing education, hiring, compliance, and . . . finally . . . marketing.

The list was not only ridiculously long, it was overwhelming.

Then it occurred to us that a 700-page, A-to-Z manual on building your investment advisory practice was not what we wanted to write and, we decided, probably not what most busy professionals wanted to read. That's because it would not only be too broad, the "very important" would invariably get watered down by the presence of the "somewhat useful."

Let's face it, when you read a book, not every page gets consumed in precisely the same way. It's our nature: Our attention and focus ebbs and flows. Our mind wanders.

So, as we evaluated our list of the things that investment advisors need to do to grow their practices, the following became obvious: We had to pare it down. Way down.

As we appraised the list, ranking and prioritizing its various assets, we started to cut and slash topics and to eliminate repetition so that little by little it began to shrink until, finally, after several days of condensing, there was only one single word left on the entire list: Marketing.

It was then we realized that we could have saved ourselves a lot of time and energy if, right from the beginning, we'd simply looked in the mirror and asked ourselves the very same question we've posed to you: What do I need to do to grow my practice?

Whenever either of us talks about our business, we both like to say, "We're not investment advisors who market, we're a marketing company that happens to be in financial services."

Upon hearing those words, some people nod with appreciation, some even chuckle, while still others stare blankly and wait for us to finish the thought, as though that can't be all there is to say on the matter.

Of course, we ourselves didn't truly understand this 20 years ago when we were just starting out, so why should someone from outside our industry understand the simple truth of that statement now?

We believe the foundation of our business is marketing: comprehensive, intensive, ongoing and focused marketing. Marketing to get new clients (sales opportunities), and then marketing to keep them (by reminding them that what you provide is not easy to replace).

In these pages we've carefully documented the specific practices and marketing campaigns that have led to our success as the co-founders and co-CEOs of, not only Hanson McClain Advisors and its almost $1.6 billion under management, but of the three other companies we have founded, one of which is now the largest reverse mortgage company in America.

So here's our promise to you: We've held nothing back. We've held nothing back because, otherwise, why bother? That's because when we researched marketing books for investment advisors, they nearly all fell into one of two categories: First there was the "general" marketing approach, and second, there was the "academic" approach.

Neither category proved particularly applicable to what we would want in a marketing book if the goal is to grow our investment advisory firm.

We decided it was time for us to write something that advisors could actually utilize to help build their practices, and we knew that if we held anything back, the entire exercise would be wasted.

In regard to that, we'd like to say the following: When it comes to marketing and growing your firm, there's no everlasting magic pill or lucky breaks, there are only the secrets you have yet to learn, and then, after you've been exposed to those, the distances you are willing to travel to accomplish your goals. With that in mind, we present to you our marketing secrets.

The rest is up to you.

SECTION 1
Advisor Marketing

"We're not just an investment advisory firm that markets. We're a marketing company that happens to be in financial services."
— Scott Hanson and Pat McClain

Marketing Overview

Marketing is a buzzword-heavy, esoteric, quasi-psychological entity with a language all its own. It's a science because it's about understanding behavior. It's an art because it's about identifying what the target audience will find appealing. In addition to all of that, marketing is imprecise because we are human and therefore prone to confusing what's creative with what's effective.

But while marketing is complex, it's also every bit as important as any other element of your practice.

Marketing encompasses advertising, branding, customer satisfaction, and much more. In that sense marketing is the process of first creating awareness and later, after that prospective client becomes a client, creating loyalty. A common mistake we see is that many advisors market to *get* the business but fail to realize they also have to market to *keep* the business.

Most of the classic definitions of marketing are too general to apply strictly to financial advisors. Yet after studying it — through both our formal and informal education, and our alliances with some of the best marketing and advertising firms around — we've found that when it comes to marketing there are only two absolutes: The process never ends and it never stops evolving.

Successful marketing will:

- Introduce you to prospective clients

- Create a steady stream of sales opportunities

- Remind prospective clients and clients about what you do and why it's valuable

- Help build customer relationships and enhance loyalty

While marketing, as you've just read, includes the continued wooing and servicing of your clients to remind them that you are there to meet their needs, in this section we're going to focus on the outreach portions of marketing and not the equally important client service and reinforcement portions, which are emphasized throughout the book in examples of best practices.

"Half our marketing budget is wasted. The problem is we don't know which half."

— Every marketing executive for the last 60 years

The Difference Between Marketing and Sales

One of the most important goals of your business should be to achieve symmetry between marketing and sales. Yet in spite of billions of dollars and thousands of hours spent trying to find this balance, even companies with household names don't always differentiate between the two. Case in point: Take the creation of almighty-sounding positions with titles like Director of Sales and Marketing, which we believe is a mistake. Don't misunderstand; we value the "Mr. Smith will see you now" influence of a powerful title — powerful titles can open doors — but while marketers focus on creating targeted messages intended to show that your firm can meet prospective client needs, sales is the intimate, usually one-on-one follow-up with the prospective client *after* marketing has caught their attention.

So while sales and marketing are strategically aligned — you might say separated at birth, even — they are not the same thing.

When it comes to sales, we value the importance of top-notch representatives because getting people to sign on the dotted line is the key to survival for every business. But for your investment advisory firm it's just as important to become a great marketer so you'll create a steady flow of new sales opportunities, and *then* to develop and implement an affirming marketing back-structure that reminds clients why they chose you in the first place.

The investment advising business is different from product-driven companies because, instead of a manufactured product, you are selling advice, guidance, confidence, and, even more so than in most any other industry, yourself. If your firm is like most small companies and your office comprises just a handful of people, then you probably wear both the marketing and sales hats. Keeping them separate in your mind's eye takes organization and focus, along with a crystal-clear understanding of the importance of their independent functions.

The "buying funnel" on the next page will help you visualize the symbiosis that exists between marketing and sales.

Notice how the funnel becomes narrower as the process evolves? While this funnel was created for companies that manufacture products like soft drinks, automobiles, or copiers, it's simple to translate the "purchase intention" segment to that of an investment advisory prospective client who is considering your firm's services. "Purchase" would be the transfer of assets, and so on.

What you want to accumulate at the bottom of this marketing and sales funnel is an ever-expanding reservoir of loyal advocates for your firm.

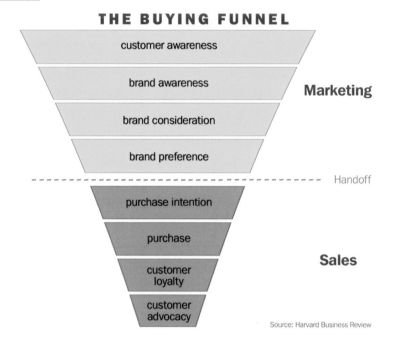

THE BUYING FUNNEL

customer awareness

brand awareness

brand consideration

brand preference

— Handoff

purchase intention

purchase

customer loyalty

customer advocacy

Marketing

Sales

Source: Harvard Business Review

Marketing Plan: Why It's Vital

"The ultimate test of an executive is his ability to write a sound marketing plan."

— Morris Hite, member, Advertising Hall of Fame

With virtually every marketing expert in the country emphasizing the importance of developing a marketing plan, it's a mystery why so many highly driven business owners never get around to creating one. A survey of investment advisors conducted by the Wharton School in June of 2009 revealed that just 58% of financial advisors had a marketing plan, and just 65% of those had *updated* that plan in the previous year.

This means only 38% of investment advisors have an updated marketing plan.

The lack of a plan is an impediment to *your* success. If your competition is part of that 38%, creating a marketing plan represents an opportunity for you to draw even with them and also get a leg up on your planless competitors.

Organizing Your Thoughts: Clear, Concise, Conceptual

Before we wrote this book, we created an outline for the messages we wanted to convey. Developing a plan is the heavy lifting of any process, and a marketing plan is as much about synthesizing your vision as it is about logistics or action. It's also important to remember that while a marketing plan is an investment that doesn't pay off overnight, it's something that should pay off over time.

In big-picture terms, your marketing plan *should* be:

- An oracle for you and your employees to rally around
- A starting point for what you want your employees to feel about your company
- A porthole into how your company works
- A tangible game plan that your employees can hold in their hands
- A document that inspires innovation, growth, and input

Narrowing it down further, your marketing plan is a living, breathing tool that should *clearly* identify such things as:

- Your overall mission
- Your target clients
- What the Heart (the emotional meaning) of your business is
- What media or PR you are going to utilize to achieve your goals

Sample Marketing Plan

In spite of their importance, and the heavy thought it takes to create one, marketing plans don't have to be overly long or complex. The following hypothetical marketing plan covers a lot of territory yet still manages to be specific.

1. Mission statement

   Be our region's go-to investment advisory firm for teachers and administrators

2. Geographical framework

   Our city, Austin, the capital of Texas, where over 22,000 current or former teachers, administrators, and staff from both local and state agencies live

3. Point of differentiation — our three terms

   Educators, local impact, helping children

4. The HEART of the matter

   Teachers change lives and we want to help them reach their retirement goals

5. Primary client target demographic

   Teachers from public and private schools

6. Secondary client target demographic

   Vested Austin School District employees who are within five years of retirement

7. Key alliance list

   - Mary Smith, Chairperson, Austin Independent School District (AISD) Board of Trustees
   - Sam Jones, Austin CFO for the Texas Education Teacher's Retirement Fund
   - Patricia Ortiz, Union Chief for AISD primary education

8. Competition

   Austin Investment Services, a 30-year-old investment advisory firm that currently handles 40% of Austin-area retirees from the Texas Education Agency (The principals at AIS will be retiring in 2014!)

9. Tactics

   ■ Product: core and differentiating offerings
   A list of all Austin-area education causes and education-centric investment opportunities

   ■ Office model (ours)
   A work environment that supports educational entities, including education-based artwork, office accessories that are education-themed, and bright red apples delivered twice a week to our office and offered to every visitor

   ■ Fee structure
   We charge a flat percentage of assets under management for clients, or $200 an hour for non-client investment advice and allocation. We donate 1.25% of profits to the following education-based nonprofits in the Austin area: (list attached)

   ■ PR: overview and media
   Our goal is to be known as the "educator's advisory firm" by forming close associations with educational entities throughout Austin and aligning our charity volunteer work and marketing efforts with teacher and administrative events, outlets, and student-centric organizations. Establish database of all districts, schools, administrative offices, nonprofits, and education-based organizations, and categorize by public, private (secular), and private (religious) status. Compile database of all educational publications,

clubs, advocacy groups, radio programs, and print and broadcast media that client demographic might read, hold membership in, or attend.

■ Control: tracking program and growth
Track inquiries regarding education and education-centric investing. The actual percentage of clients who **want** *allocation in education-based industries and investments. Total commissions delivered to charities (as percentage of total). Media mentions in* Teacher and Administrator Magazine, *the education section of the* Austin Daily Star, Teachers United Weekly Magazine, *and* School Employees *biweekly newspaper.*

It's human nature to believe that bigger is always better, but if you want to grow your advisory firm, it probably won't happen if you market to everyone. Developing a marketing plan around a dedicated niche-client demographic should result in sustained growth in nearly all economic environments. Expansion and "arteries of growth" (inroads into still other niches) will naturally occur from a consistent and ongoing "narrowcast" beginning.

Branding

"In this ever-changing society, the most powerful and enduring brands are built from the heart."
— Howard Schultz, CEO of Starbucks

Brand: *to mark with a branding iron, to burn.*

Your brand is the impression you have "burned" into people's perceptions through marketing, advertising, and perhaps most importantly, word of mouth (customer advocacy). Your brand is what separates you and your practice from everyone else. In that sense, branding isn't any one thing that you do but is, instead, the result of everything you do which results in an impression.

There's a big difference between branding for a service (you as an investment advisor) and branding for a product (Coke). For a product, branding is actually the main goal of marketing. Every Coke, McDonald's hamburger, and cup of Starbucks coffee will be exactly the same. The absolute certainty that you can order *and receive* a consistent, desirable product eliminates the anxiety that comes with the *potential* for disappointment.

Conversely, as an investment advisor, you are selling a service. To a great extent, service is subjective. Your overarching goal is that, by exceeding the needs of your clients, the brand association of your firm is so positive that you limit negative subjective opinions.

Scott Goodson, author of the book *Strawberry Frog,* wrote in the May 27, 2012, edition of *Forbes Magazine,* "Looking out into the world today, it's easy to see why brands are more important now than at any time in the past 100 years. Brands are psychology and science brought together as a 'promise mark' as opposed to a trademark."

In our society we value consistent certainties every bit as much as we do quality.

But there is some debate about the value of branding, especially

WORD OF MOUTH

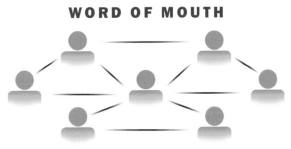

Source: Hanson McClain Advisors

Consistent branding results in strong word-of-mouth advocacy.

for small, regional firms. The thinking is that if you have a limited budget or are just starting out, it's probably not cost-effective to focus on image.

To this we say … sort of. Here's the rub: While parts of branding are achieved through marketing and messaging — and will cost you time and money — it bears repeating that the most effective branding is the byproduct of providing consistently good service.

As an investment advisor, should branding *ever* be your over-arching goal?

Yes. But primarily in the context of the specific tools we are going to present. Because what is the staying power of being flashy? Can you name even one ad from last year's Super Bowl? And each of those companies is a household name.

With consumer goods, which can often be purchased online right after a television ad airs, there's value in attention-grabbing advertisements for one-time events. But when it comes to investment advising, a great day means nothing. It's imperative to be consistent day after day, week after week, year after year.

Brand Logo

Logo: *a name, symbol, or trademark designed for easy recognition or identification*

Milton Glaser, one of the best known graphic designers of the 20th century, said, "The logo is the entry point to the brand." Who are we to argue with the man who designed the famous logo below?

An effective logo can create a feeling of dedication and emotion even in people who've never seen it before. (Color, shape, and design all speak to memory and emotional experience.) Your logo is your company's face. When it comes to creating one, consider the guidelines below.

- Ensure it incorporates a strong image with no clutter.
- Make it easy to read and recognize at a glance.
- Use graphics that are appropriate for our industry (safe and strong).
- Select one that works well with your company name.
- Make sure it clearly communicates your business (not always possible).
- Test that it looks good in several mediums, including your website, advertising, business cards.
- Have versions for use that look good in black and white, as well as in color.

Here's an admission: When we first founded Hanson McClain Advisors, we didn't have a logo. We knew investing, not graphic design. It took a couple of months to create one, and in a way, our business was fortunate to survive, as we'd both made the mistake of believing that hard work and investment expertise would conquer all.

It didn't then and it doesn't now.

Creating Your Logo
(And Just About Anything Else That Takes Design Expertise)

Logo design takes creative software mastery. If your budget permits and you have no in-house design wizard, we encourage you to pursue bids from local firms. We are in a relationship business, and you want working partnerships with talented local designers who will grow along with you.

Your goal is a logo that announces who you are so that every time someone sees it they know right away it's your firm.

Hanson McClain Advisors
Independent Investment Advice

New Firms and Cash Flow Considerations

When we first opened our doors, cash flow was a serious consideration. If you can't afford to hire a graphic designer, there are some reasonable options. First, contact the local college, junior college, or art school and speak with someone in the art department. Ask whether designing a logo could be a graphic design class project or a contest with a cash award. A few hundred dollars should provide incentive for students to compete.

To close the deal, emphasize any connection you have to the college, and mention that you are a *local firm* looking to utilize *local talent.*

A quick aside about working with artists: Young designers are more likely to want to reshape the world (and your logo) in their own image. To get a world class logo (and perhaps launch a career in the process), you need to *clearly* articulate what your firm does: "We offer consistent service and careful investment advice." Articulate what your firm doesn't do, as well: "We don't provide Las Vegas–style entertainment."

Not the type who wants to query the local college for a graphic designer? Where just a generation ago you might be stuck with a logo created by an inexperienced relative or neighbor, those days are gone forever. Companies such as 99designs provide electronic access to literally thousands of talented graphic designers, with results that are usually fast and cost-effective. 99designs is run like a contest. Simply go to the website, register, create a quick "design brief" that outlines what you need (website, logo, etc.) and how much you'll pay (prices can start around $200, but the more you pay, the more options you'll have), and within about a week you should have several designs to choose from.

Online resources that are reliable, convenient, inexpensive, and fast are not limited to graphic design. You can now locate and solicit *professionals* to write such things as white papers, newsletters, or ad campaigns, and you can even easily find focus groups to give you unbiased feedback on those very same campaigns, providing you with a service that used to be available only to companies with very large budgets.

Branding: This Is What You Should Do in the Next 30 Days

- Create (or reassess) your logo.

- Apply it to business cards, letterhead, and invoices.

- Set up an email address that includes your firm name.

- Create a website. (As with the logo, there's lots of inexpensive, creative help on Craigslist and at local art and graphic design schools.)

- Reassess your mission statement.

The Difference Between Branding and Advertising

"Advertising is the burn, branding is the scar."
— Pat McClain

Your brand is the impression people have when they hear your firm's name or see your logo, whereas advertising is a message intended to build your brand. Both branding and advertising are part of marketing. The problem with advertising in the financial services sector is that the acceptable messaging of our industry is extremely limited by compliance considerations.

The struggle between marketing and compliance is an important one. We have an in-house compliance department and they are tough, which is great for our practice. In any dynamic firm, you have a tug-of-war between marketing and compliance (with marketing swinging doors open and compliance slamming them shut). This struggle actually serves both the best interests of your firm and the public, because it creates restrictions for carpetbaggers looking to exploit investors and, by industry association, damage your brand.

Advertising

Advertising: *the act or practice of calling attention to one's product*

Effective advertising creates a feeling that motivates action. That feeling can be confidence, fear, excitement, urgency, or need. Advertising is expensive, which puts small advisory firms at a competitive disadvantage.

We don't create our advertising in-house — we *manage* it in-house — but experience has taught us that in-house advertising tends to become less effective over time. This is because the emotional connection to the company doesn't allow the employee (or even the owners) to see the firm in an artistic light.

Methods of Advertising

While we've utilized just about every form of advertising known to our industry, and while our marketing approach continues to evolve (we're using more video, for one thing), our traditional advertising is found almost exclusively in regional magazines, neighborhood newspapers, and on the radio.

In an industry where word of mouth is king and compliance concerns dictate content, commercial advertising — while an entrenched part of our approach — has proven to be a less cost-effective resource for client procurement than some of the tools we'll cover here.

It's a catch-22: Most small investment advisory firms simply can't afford — nor would they find it particularly cost-effective — to break the bank with advertising, and yet there are only so many channels to build brand awareness and rise above the noise.

Here are some targeted advertising suggestions, with bigger picture, ongoing master marketing tasks to come:

- Target radio ads *before* and *after* other FA's radio shows.
- Advertise in neighborhood newspapers.
- Utilize your city's business journals and magazines.
- Place notices in church bulletins. (We've had surprising success with this inexpensive method.)

Advertising Limitations

The vibrant magazine advertisement below has a color photograph depicting a positive message, but a testimonial for Hanson McClain Advisors is nowhere to be found. You can't endorse your firm, nor can you utilize client endorsements in your advertising materials, and this reduces their effectiveness for brand awareness. The strength of the ad isn't derived from content — though there's usable information and a pleasing presentation — it's actually the ad's physical existence on the page and prominent placement in the magazine that represents its true value to our bottom line.

As we've repeated throughout this book and section, while marketing is essential to your success, and while advertising is

Full page ad from January 2013 *Sacramento Magazine*.

an integral part of marketing, it's the day-to-day performance margins — the repetitive service nuances — that are going to make the difference in the success of your business.

Publicity

"If a young man tells his date she's intelligent, looks lovely, and is a great conversationalist, he's saying the right things to the right person and that's marketing. If the young man tells his date how handsome, smart and successful he is — that's advertising. If someone else tells the young woman how handsome, smart and successful her date is — that's publicity."

— S.H. Simmons, author and humorist

Publicity is the art of getting *others* to talk about your company in a positive way.

While general news publicity is almost impossible to direct demographically, it's free except for the time and energy, and it provides great exposure. One of the best ways to create positive publicity is through community involvement. As you'll read later, we are heavily engaged in our community, and that engagement has resulted in significant amounts of attention directed toward our firm from throughout the region.

Press Releases

Announcements of special events and awards and charitable sponsorships and news about company expansions, office relocations, and personnel changes are all excellent reasons to blast press releases out to both local and national media. Write the releases yourself and have an intern send them. Many industry outlets (*InvestmentNews*, for one) regularly publish announcements of the comings and goings of firm personnel, but you have to notify them via press release and hope your announcement is used. Consistent, ongoing attempts at PR should result in exposure and greater brand recognition.

There are successful firms that purport to do little or no advertising and instead rely almost exclusively on publicity for exposure, so channeling an increasing portion of your marketing efforts toward publicity could significantly raise your profile while adding little or no cost to your bottom line.

For immediate release ...

HMSA's Matt Russell Awarded
Sac Biz Journal's CFO of the Year

Sacramento, CA, July 30th, 2012, 10:05 am

Hanson McClain Strategic Advisors of Sacramento, California, is pleased to announce that our own Matt Russell has been named the *Sacramento Business Journal's* CFO of the Year for 2012.

During a July 13th awards ceremony at the Sheraton Grand Sacramento, Russell was honored in front of an estimated 300 attendees from Sacramento's business, government and nonprofit sectors. The Sacramento Business Journal's awards committee considered several criteria in deciding the winner, including leadership, community service, and contributions to the firm. During Russell's four years at Hanson McClain he's made numerous proactive alterations to the company's financial structure which have drastically cut costs and subsequently freed up revenue for investment in expansion. In fact, so much is thought of Russell's contributions to the firm that in February of 2012 he was named Pres-

HMSA CFO Matt Russell

ident of HMSA and will oversee two major growth initiatives which will be introduced later this month.

"Matt's a team player and consistently makes decisions that greatly benefit the firm," said HMSA Co-founder, Pat McClain. "Scott (HMSA Co-founder, Scott Hanson) and I are extremely pleased and believe that people will be hearing much more from Matt and from HMSA in the coming months."

(To view the entire Sacramento Business Journal article on Matt Russell, please click on the photo to the left.)

HMSA's Sacramento Office
Source: Sacramento Business Journal

###

CONTACT: HMA President Steve Burnett
Hanson McClain Advisors
8775 Folsom Blvd., Suite #100, Sacramento, CA 95826
Phone: (800) 482-2196 www.hansonmcclain.com

HMSA

A sample press release from 2012.

Publicity: What You Should Do Immediately

- Create a press release template with your company's logo.
- Compile a database and "blast" email announcements to media outlets using Constant Contact or another list management service. Important: Paste the announcements in the body of the email. Attachments may be discarded unread.
- From your master list, create a list of local media — specifically, your local newspaper's and magazine's business columnists — and target them to build relationships.
- Subscribe to outlets such as HARO (helpareporter.com). Journalists and bloggers from nearly every media outlet in the country utilize HARO to locate experts for stories. The alerts arrive daily via email. Have an associate or intern monitor the announcements each morning to respond to appropriate query matches.

The Five Master Marketing Tasks for Investment Advisors

Whether you are just starting out or have been an investment advisor for many years, in addition to creating, implementing, and following a marketing plan, here are five master marketing tasks that we strongly suggest you incorporate into your arsenal.

1. Get on the radio!

2. Write articles.

3. Write a book.

4. Publish quarterly newsletters.

5. Send out quarterly mailers.

Get on the Radio!

We've hosted a call-in financial news radio show for over 18 years, and it has been an *important* component in our success. Rarely does a day go by when we don't get at least one prospective client phone call or web inquiry from someone who first heard of us through our Money Matters program.

In the context of our firm, what exactly does important mean? In 2012, the year we accepted the most new clients in Hanson McClain Advisors company history, 20% of our new clients came to us because of our radio program, which places it second only to referrals as our most important new client resource.

This chart shows not only the magnitude of what that 20% represents for our company but also, just as importantly, what it says about the effectiveness of hosting a radio program. And to underscore the importance of radio, a decade ago our radio program was responsible for almost 40% of our new clients.

Quite simply, the impact of our radio program on the growth of our retail advisory business is almost impossible to exaggerate.

How Radio Can Impact Your Firm

A weekly radio presence offers you several professional marketing advantages over print and traditional radio advertising, all in one unique platform. Radio's advantages include:

- A consistent outlet for brand awareness
- An unhurried, extended stage to showcase expertise
- A platform to create a following (we regularly get referrals from non-client listeners)
- The ability to demonstrate your durability, longevity, commitment, and credibility
- The creation of a personal connection with listeners and prospective clients
- A valuable service for people who may not need an advisor

Paying to Play on Radio

A majority of local weekend radio programming is paid for by the program host or sponsor (called "pay to play") and utilized as a marketing platform with the cost ranging from outrageous (hundreds of thousands of dollars per year) to affordable (a few thousand dollars per year) depending on the regional market. Because some markets may have less professional expertise available to them than elsewhere, it's not altogether impossible to find a hosting opportunity *for free* — but it's unlikely.

Working Your Way onto the Air

Contact the marketing department of each target station. As a result of deregulation, practically all the stations in one region *might* be owned by the same company, but contact them anyway. Inquire about listener demographics and slot availability. Obviously, as an investment advisor you'll want a station with a mature listenership.

If the local airwaves are overrun with financial shows, you're going to want to develop a reputation that differentiates you from the noise of the hosts who are merely promoting investment products or themselves. Position yourself as the "helpful" advisor, the "investor advocate," or the "retirement expert."

SOURCE OF NEW HMA CLIENTS, 2012

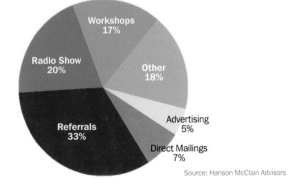

Workshops 17%

Radio Show 20%

Other 18%

Referrals 33%

Advertising 5%

Direct Mailings 7%

Source: Hanson McClain Advisors

Follow these tips for a successful radio show:

- Avoid getting stuck between financial shows hosted by un-ethical advisors.
- Develop various hooks such as a weekly top ten.
- Utilize interesting bumper music (theme music used before and after breaks).
- Have an affable partner or a consistent stream of co-hosts or guests.
- Use the platform and your expertise *to serve and not to promote* (it's not an infomercial).
- Attract the broadest possible audience (unlike your practice) to maximize ratings, referrals, callers, brand awareness, and possible advertisers.

After you have a contact in the marketing department of your target station, pitch your program. You will need to prepare several show topics in advance. If no slots are available or you can't afford the fees, then you need to get creative.

The important thing is to get on the air.

Pat McClain (*left*) and Scott Hanson taping KFBK's *Money Matters*.

Radio for Beginners

While the benefits are difficult to overstate, radio is expensive. This is especially true in the major media centers (New York, Chicago, Los Angeles, and the San Francisco Bay Area) that have loads of competitors in line ahead of you, all of whom are willing to pay top dollar for the available hours.

There are ways around these obstacles. First, find another local advisor and offer to share a slot. This would cut your hosting fee in half. You can alternate weeks as main host and co-host, or, if you are willing to let them take the lead, you may start out as the sidekick and lower your costs even more.

No partner in sight? Find someone who already has a program and ask about becoming a recurring guest. To enhance the possibility, become a top-down expert on their show. Find the information gap in their program and then invent a way to fill it. Add value. Investment advisors understand bottom lines, but that doesn't mean they are familiar with the needs of their listeners or the nuances of their marketplace. Approach them from the perspective of enhancing their product, and they may be willing to form an alliance.

Another way to get on the air is to find a non-financial news program, and then approach the host about doing a weekly one-minute segment. Find a show that focuses on real estate or consumer advocacy, and then ask about doing a weekly market update. You are seeking to gain access and add value at little or no cost to you.

Write Articles

You need more than just good verbal skills to be a successful investment advisor. Much of what we do revolves around the nuanced dissemination of the personal information of clients and business partners, as well as careful communication with various oversight entities. This correspondence will exist forever in either hard copy or electronic format.

If you simply can't bring yourself to write a coherent letter or marketing piece, you'd be well-advised to make certain that someone in your office can. Poorly written communications are red flags and make a universally terrible impression.

While large regional newspapers are in decline, neighborhood newspapers are both thriving *and engaged* in a perpetual quest to produce content that is inexpensive but also relevant to their readers. We are often approached about writing columns for papers — and have done so on several occasions — including a nine-year stint as a weekly columnist for the *Sacramento Bee*.

Finding Media Outlets for Your Articles

Make a list of every newspaper (large and small) within a 50-mile radius. You'll be surprised how many daily, weekly, monthly, and bimonthly outlets exist. Identify your targets and then contact the editor or publisher and ask about submitting a guest column or article. Remember, this is not a promotional piece for your firm but a platform for you to increase brand awareness. Again, how can you add value? Present a well-researched topic that explores or explains a timely interest of their (and your) target audience.

Sample newspaper articles:

- The importance of participating in your company's defined contribution 401(k), 403(b) or 457 plan
- Analysis of Social Security or Medicare
- Ten questions to ask your financial advisor
- The ins and outs of emotional investing
- Market cycles throughout history and the value of staying the course

Write a Book

In 2006 we released *Money Matters: Essential Tips & Tools for Building Financial Peace of Mind*. Written for consumers, *Money Matters* contains tips and advice on handling debt, real estate, taxes, and investments. The format is concise, with each topic covered in three paragraphs or less.

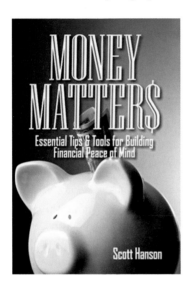

It's been several years since the release of *Money Matters*, and yet we still receive requests for review copies, and we strategically display the book throughout our offices.

Whether you or someone in your office is a seasoned writer or you need to collaborate with an outside agency, writing a book can enhance your brand. A professionally produced book will provide you with increased credibility while also giving you a versatile, *authoritative* marketing tool that can be used for everything from workshop giveaways to gifts for clients to inclusion in media kits.

Some Specifics for Bringing a Book to Print

As with the marketing plan, home in on your audience and narrow your message. Create an outline consisting of 10–12 primary chapters about big-picture concerns, *and then* divide each chapter down into 8–10 workable subheadings, each of which is a concise cure for the big-picture chapter heading.

The majority of the content for these workable subheadings should be no more than a few paragraphs long.

Dividing the book this way not only makes the writing process easier, it creates a reader-friendly reference piece with a hundred small lessons rather than one large one. As for the writing process, just 15 minutes a day will result in significant progress towards the completion of this substantial master marketing tool.

Here's an example of a single chapter outline:

1. Debt management
   - Five little known causes of debt
   - Ten monthly expenses you don't need
   - Good versus bad debt
   - Tips for managing credit cards
   - Should I borrow from my 401(k) to pay off debt?
   - Should I use the equity in my house?
   - Three ways to consolidate debt
   - Ten ways to cut expenses
   - How to save $1,000 every month

Considering your education and expertise, most of you reading these words could probably write the chapter outlined above with minimal research.

Get Assistance

Still not sure you can write a book alone? Craigslist is full of writers looking for work. If you can create an outline and provide guidance, there are competent professionals out there who would love to help you fill in the gaps.

Lastly, because the goal is to create an attractive tool that serves your marketing interests while also providing useful content for the reader, hiring a book packager to take the project "home" — create the cover, proofread, format, arrange the printing, and possibly even do some PR — is a good way to go. To keep expenses down, you could initially sponsor a small printing (100–200 copies) while making the book available in an e-format, and *later* print additional hard copies for distribution purposes as needed.

Book Plan

- Identify your target audience (when it comes to a general release book, broader is better).
- Create your topic (spend time online and at the local bookstore researching potential subjects).
- Create an outline: 8–10 chapters (problems), each with 8–10 subheadings (cures).
- Create a budget: What are you willing to spend?
- Contact some book packagers and see what they offer (prices vary from extreme to affordable).
- If you have difficulty writing, or can't find the time, locate a local ghostwriter.

Publish Quarterly Newsletters

We write our own quarterly newsletter, but at one time we did what many small advisory firms do: We contracted with an outside service to provide content. As we grew, we determined that we could bring the creative process in-house while at the same time personalizing and controlling every aspect of the process and message.

Producing a newsletter takes time and expertise, but because it's an excellent way to enhance brand awareness, build credibility, and strengthen relationships by "touching" clients, it remains a staple of our marketing arsenal.

As with many of the tools we've introduced here, a newsletter has what we call "tentacles." (Imagine a long, varied and flexible reach.) Each quarter we write a five-page newsletter, and we use a local partner to print and mail over 1,000 hard copies. We then send out over 6,000 copies via email to clients, prospective clients, and select members of the media. We display the latest edition in our lobbies and make them available to our custodians.

While the tentacles of a professionally written newsletter with

Hanson McClain Advisors Investment Newsletter

JANUARY 2013

Abraham Lincoln and the Fiscal Cliff

Inside This Edition:

One need only look back at history to realize how things haven't changed that much over time. Take angry political rhetoric: Seven score and ten years ago, Abraham Lincoln delivered the Gettysburg Address, which proved beyond the shadow of a doubt that he was a poor writer, lacked an insightful wit and was an uninspiring public speaker. (Or so his political opponents said.)

On November 6th, 2012, America held its 57th quadrennial presidential election. For months leading up to November, candidates Romney and Obama launched attacks against each other in an attempt to gain political advantage. Some called the run-up to the 2012 election the most negative in U.S. history.

But how did it compare to the discourse of previous eras? For a noteworthy example, we need look no further than the aspersions cast between close friends George Washington and Thomas Jefferson.

By the late 1700s, America found itself tens of millions of dollars in debt to Great Britain, in part because the British manufactured the machinery that Americans wanted but couldn't afford to buy. Establishing a tradition that continues today, we just kept right on ordering the machinery anyway.

Then, as now, many saw massive debt as a threat to liberty. Yet despite intense opposition, in 1794 George Washington proceeded to sign the controversial "Jay Treaty," which not only made America even more economically dependent on Great Britain, it moved us away from our Revolutionary War ally France. In response to the treaty, Jefferson publicly denounced fellow Founding Father George Washington for endangering America through a lethal combination of British favoritism and senility. While the country survived, Washington and Jefferson never spoke again.

200 Years Ago	1
HMA Year in Review	3
Market Indices	5

If you'd like to automatically receive an electronic copy of our quarterly newsletter, visit us at www.hansonmcclain.com

3620 Fair Oaks Blvd.
Suite 300
Sacramento, CA 95864

(800) 482-2196

www.hansonmcclain.com

Hanson McClain Advisors
Independent Investment Advice

Cover of January 2013 HMA Newsletter.

a narrative style and topical content extend well beyond anything we can easily quantify, it's a terrific serial marketing piece that combines elements of the radio program, quarterly mailers, traditional advertising, and even the book, all in an easy-to-digest format. If you want to keep costs to a minimum, we suggest you create an email template and make your first newsletters specifically electronic. Eventually, however, you will want to create hard copies which will invariably end up in unpredictable locations (waiting rooms in medical offices, for instance) where it could take as little as one new client to make the entire process cost-effective.

Send Out Quarterly Mailers

In 2012, 7% of our new clients came to us through quarterly mailers like the one below. We utilize a local service to compile a mailing list with a specific target demographic (say, people between the ages of 55 and 75), and who live in the four most populous counties in our region. We then create the content and send out as many as 20,000 in one mailing.

While not inexpensive — expenses include the mailing list, distributor, postage, and materials — quarterly mailers have served us well. Our typical 7% success rate pays for the process and, as with any physical marketing material, whether book, newsletter, or mailer, we've come to assume that both the mailer's reach and impact exceed the *measurable* 7% that mailers added to our bottom line in 2012.

While your budget, particular market, and unique client niche demographic will all factor into your marketing and advertising decisions, the five master marketing tasks presented here have proven to be highly effective, big-picture builders of our firm. Each has extensive reach, and each meets a number of the ongoing marketing goals that should matter to you.

Closing Thoughts: Marketing with Video

We increasingly utilize video, not only as a means to reach current clients, but also as a way to personalize communications and materials that are intended for prospective clients.

In addition to creating our "New Client Welcome Video" and various informational pieces, we've begun augmenting our *written*

Hanson McClain Advisors
Independent Investment Advice

February 14, 2013

Dear FIRST:

Is your investment portfolio performing the way you'd like? It's nearly two full months into 2013, which means *right now* is the ideal time to ask yourself if your current investment advisor is meeting your specific needs.

Nationally recognized by *Barron's*[1] magazine, and with offices in Sacramento, Roseville and Folsom, we're Scott Hanson and Pat McClain of Hanson McClain Advisors and we'd like to help you make *and keep* a New Year's resolution to better manage your financial future.

The first thing we recommend is that you thoroughly assess your current advisor. Does he or she listen to your concerns, or do they speak in the "language of finance" and then just brush your worries aside? Because when it comes to retirement, there's no "one size fits all." You're unique and so are your investment objectives.

Whether you're planning to retire in the next few years, or have already left the workforce, our credentialed advisors have the expertise, experience and acumen to help familiarize you with the possibilities for balancing and diversifying your portfolio. Our mission is to provide you with the confidence that comes from being *clearly* understood, and then to work with you to create a strategy that helps you meet your investment goals both now and in the future.

So contact us today at 1-888-2HANSON for a complimentary portfolio check-up, or visit us at HansonMcClain.com.

Sincerely,

Scott Hanson, CFP®, CFS®, ChFC   Pat McClain, ChFC

Tune to Hanson McClain Advisors' Money Matters on KFBK Newstalk AM 1530 Saturdays from 10-11:00 a.m. and Sundays 2-3:00 p.m.

[1] Published in August 2012: Barron's 2012 Top 100 Independent Financial Advisors. Barron's© magazine is a trademark of Dow Jones L.P. The ranking reflects volume of assets overseen by the advisors/teams, revenues generated for firms and the quality of advisors' practices.

Hanson McClain Advisors is an Investment Advisor registered with the Securities and Exchange Commission. 02/13

Quarterly mailer from February 2013.

advisor biographies with video biographies that we record in a controlled film studio. Every three months, to coincide with the release of our quarterly newsletter, we create a quarterly webcast where the principals and officers of our firm discuss market events and other pertinent financial topics. These webcasts are available in the Knowledge Center we've created on our website at www. hansonmcclain.com.

The reasons for the increase in our use of video are straightforward: prospective clients who are perusing our website or marketing materials are, as much as anything, seeking a connection. Video puts a human face on the investment advisor selection process. While we appreciate the specificity of the written word, video adds a unique dimension to our marketing content. A prospective client researching our firm is more likely to make the initial phone call if they feel a connection to an individual, which a well-crafted video can facilitate. Additionally, in our 20 years as investment advisors, it's become apparent that there are people who simply will never read *any* marketing piece but will gladly watch a video if the topic has relevance to their plans or interests. Lastly, with smart phone technology, anyone, anywhere in the world, can instantly watch our content, meaning video has a reach and a power to influence and inform that was unthinkable just a generation ago.

A Brief Video Warning

Video production takes expertise and experience — on both sides of the camera. Of the marketing tools presented in this section, video is by far the most difficult to perfect. In fact, while we consider it a vital component of our marketing approach, we consider it more of a facilitator than an independent tool.

The reality is that not every advisor is ideal for this medium, and a poorly executed video could negatively impact your marketing efforts and undermine your credibility. Even with professional production, video takes both commitment and preparation, so don't allow yourself to be sold on either its merits or its modernity until you have a well-crafted message and are absolutely comfortable with the content (namely, yourself) that you present.

SECTION 2
Community Involvement

"Great charitable or business partnerships are a lot like great mar-
riages: you quickly realize that building upon agreements is much
more important than standing your ground over differences."
— Scott Hanson

Two decades ago, with a client-centric approach and the promise to make community involvement a cornerstone of our practice, we founded Hanson McClain Advisors. The workload that comes with building a company is extensive, but as we grew, our commitment to the community grew right along with us.

A couple of years after founding Hanson McClain, something interesting happened: Our understanding of the possibilities of volunteerism matured.

This maturation came to light during our annual end-of-year review, when the conversation turned to the number of clients that had come to us through our charity work. For the first time it dawned on us that there was a significant intersection between our business and our social involvement. No matter how you looked at it, serving the community was absolutely ideal for everyone: It was good for the charity and the people it supported; good for the community at large; good for both of us personally; and — because our work with charities had evolved to where we had assumed leadership positions, meeting prospective clients in the process — our volunteer work was good for our business. And as you'll soon read, it was good for our employees as well.

It was *that* day when we realized for the first time that community involvement is the perfect avocation.

The Intersection Between Giving and Your Practice

"A bit of fragrance always clings to the hand that gives the rose."
— Chinese Proverb

To a lot of people the word "charity" is synonymous with "purity." It is to us, as well. But the purity of an action need not be diminished simply because that action benefits the principals in different ways. Yes, we'd both been involved in community service in college, which was long before we realized that our volunteer service could benefit anything *except* the charity. We were both raised to believe, and continue to believe, that volunteerism is, for its own sake, a most worthwhile endeavor.

The fact is that charities need you. Most depend on the largesse of private business for their existence. But it's not only about the money you can give. As a financial advisor, you possess many of the intangible talents (quantitative reasoning, recruitment

Valerie and Scott Hanson received the Salvation Army Spirit of Caring award for 2011.

experience, management skill, familiarity with budgets) that are in short supply at many charitable organizations.

Conversely, from the perspective of the charity, when it comes to the perception of the motivations behind giving, be it the chairman of the board or a four-hour-per-week volunteer, most people appreciate the complexity of the relationship that exists between charitable entity and benefactor.

Again, everybody wins.

The bottom line is that we encourage you to give of yourself with the best of intentions, and later, when you and your firm invariably benefit from the association, you can humbly receive those blessings without guilt or trepidation.

Weathering Criticism

We're going to briefly jump ahead here to talk about your reputation. One lesson we've repeated throughout the book is how each decision you make should be made through the lens of your core values. Another lesson we emphasize throughout the book is how you need to create strong, favorable, and unique brand associations.

All things being equal, if you utilize your core values to make decisions, create key brand associations, and are client-centric at all times, you are putting your practice in a position to surpass the competition.

Yet while all this is absolutely essential, if you plateau there, that seemingly admirable level of execution is not going to be enough for you to realize sustained success. Here's why:

Let's just *assume* that the focus of your business is predicated upon meeting the needs of your clients. And yet despite a perfect track record of fiduciary service to those clients, you've become the target of an anonymous smear campaign on the review website Yelp by an individual who claims you have repeatedly failed to provide good customer service.

Now, naturally, if an *existing* client complains directly to you or to a member of your team, you immediately take every necessary step to address and correct the problem, and in the process you and your staff transform an angry client into a fan for life.

A direct complaint can be easily solved.

But what can you do to fight back against the type of attack that we'll call "free-floating criticism"?

Free-floating criticism is nothing like a phone call, personal letter, or email; it may be a rumor or even the musings of an unhappy crackpot. Yet while often anonymous and, hopefully, unfounded, the problem is that free-floating criticism continues to live on the Internet and may never go away.

The Vulnerable Reputation

Over time, the continued existence of free-floating criticism damages the lifeblood of your business. Like termites in a house's walls, it slowly devours your superstructure and causes serious injury to your brand.

Sure, your very best clients know that you're terrific, but your *prospective clients* do not. In fact, the means by which prospective clients can assess your character *and business practices* are exceedingly few. The reality is that unless free-floating negative attacks are rendered impotent or even laughable by an entrenched community sentiment that is *overwhelmingly* positive, even *highly suspect* Internet reviews that are poorly written or lacking specifics can set your practice back in ways that can be difficult to overcome.

The Preemptive Response

It's not as though you can simply obliterate free-floating criticism on sites such as Yelp by *reactively* posting a few glowing endorsements beneath the complaint. (The SEC and FINRA are very clear about what constitutes advertising and such posts aren't worth the risk.)

In the financial services sector, you've got to be intensely *proactive* because the *reactive* damage-control model is full of limitations. With that in mind, preventing or disarming free-floating criticism is only possible when your community knows about the core values of your firm. This means that, to make your brand less permeable to negativity, you need extensive "everybody wins" charity involvement.

Don't Ignore the Word on the Street (Or on the Information Highway)

When it comes to the effects of online reviews, a 2012 *Wall Street Journal* article on the power of Yelp to impact customer opinion yielded some interesting data: First, Yelp is one of the top-50 websites in America, and second, due to the workings of its proprietary algorithms, *negative reviews* are given a preferential ranking over positive ones. Simply put, people searching for information about your company may see negative comments first.

Studies *specific* to the financial services industry are lacking,

Runners gather at the starting line at the November 2011 Run to Feed the Hungry, an annual event in Sacramento, California.

but studies of the impact *negative* reviews have on businesses have shown that, from doctors to restaurants, bad reviews can cost a business as much as 20% or more of revenue.

But that's only the beginning.

Google is the #1 website in the world. When you begin a Google search by entering, for example, the words "Denver financial advisors," Google no longer just compiles a top-ten list of the most popular websites that match that description.

It used to, but no longer.

Google now utilizes its own sophisticated algorithms which, purportedly, are capable of locating negative information *anywhere on the Internet*. When your business receives a bad review on Yelp (or, presumably, on Facebook), the search engine Google — sensitive about being seen as endorsing companies with poor business practices — *automatically* moves your website further and further down its search order until, if enough negative information is found, it may actually delete your company from its search results.

Being absent from Google would be the equivalent of your firm disappearing from the entire phone book in 1980.

While there are a number of reasons why the potential impact of free-floating criticism should concern you, here's our most compelling: A recent Hanson McClain Advisors internal audit revealed that roughly 16% of *total visitors* found their way to our website after entering "Sacramento financial advisors" in Google, Bing, or Yahoo. Currently, when a prospective client enters "Sacramento financial advisors" into a search engine, Hanson McClain Advisors is the first independent practice that appears on the page. Because our name is at the top of the list, we get the first opportunity to make an impression.

What if one negative Yelp review becomes two or even three? Can your business withstand three negative reviews? How about four or five? Can you afford to drop from first to fifth or even off Google entirely?

The first question is, where precisely would your practice be without a supportive community and with no Google referrals? Which leads us to the second question, where precisely *could* your practice be with a client-centric approach, published core values, numerous positive Yelp reviews, and an unrivaled reputation for community involvement?

"You make a living by what you get. You make a life by what you give."
— Winston Churchill

Evidence That Your Involvement Is Working

Your reputation isn't measured purely by dollars under management. Conversely, you can't leave the fate of your company in the hands of rogue Internet reviewers, some of whom may actually be your competition. Your current clients may indeed admire and respect you, but the fact is that many of those clients will keep that appreciation to themselves.

Here's a recent example of how our brand has made inroads into the consciousness of the community at large:

> In the spring of 2012 we hired "Jack" from Oakland. Jack was looking to rent a house in Sacramento and found a place on an Internet real estate site that matched his needs.
>
> The next morning Jack arrived at the property for a tour, but by 9:00 a.m. there were already more than a dozen people inside viewing the house.
>
> In spite of the presence of so many others, Jack waded through, took a tour, and liked what he saw. So he filled out a rental application and handed it back to the agent.

As Jack got back in his car, he thought, "Well, that's the end of that."

Almost immediately his cell phone rang. It was the rental agent asking if he would come back inside. Jack figured he'd made a mistake on the application.

When he went back, however, the agent walked up and offered him the property.

"Why me?" asked Jack.

The agent asked, "Do you work for Hanson McClain?"

Jack nodded that he did.

"That's enough for me," said the agent.

This story is an indication that the combination of good business practices, a customer-centric approach, extensive community service, good hires, core values, luck, and a host of other factors both large and small are symbiotically shaping opinion.

The contents of *Investment Advisor Marketing* are intended to help you *maintain* your footing as you traverse the path toward management of a billion-plus dollars. And as our two decades of experience, combined with the contents of this section, show, that path *absolutely* includes community involvement.

The Value of Community Involvement

- It helps individuals.
- It helps the community.
- It's emotionally satisfying.
- It expands your business.
- It helps protect your brand.
- It makes your employees feel a part of something larger than themselves.

Measuring Your Level of Community Involvement

"Don't say you don't have enough time. You have exactly the same number of hours per day that were given to Helen Keller, Pasteur, Michelangelo, Mother Teresa, Leonardo da Vinci, Thomas Jefferson, and Albert Einstein."

— H. Jackson Brown, Jr., writer

Like most advisors, you probably categorize your clients based on the amount of money they've invested with you. It's only logical that, for the sake of organization, you divide your clients into groups (such as A, B, C, D, Gold, Silver, Platinum, etc.). Each group may require a different level of service.

When it comes to community involvement, think of your commitment to service in the same way: The more you give to a charity, the more they get from you. Conversely, the greater the personal and professional benefits you reap, as well.

Let's start by introducing what we call the "levels of commitment." But unlike with clients, rather than ranking your commitment monetarily — by money donated — we've found that, when it comes to involvement, *time and expertise* are actually more valuable and have greater influence than "mere" monetary contribution. In short, we want you to measure your commitment by activity.

We're going to help you rate yourself and then explain where you want to be, and why.

First Level Involvement

First-level commitment occurs when you give a charity a financial contribution. While there's nothing wrong with a photo op of you handing a check to the COO of a charity, let's look at this in another way:

When you were growing up did you have a relative who, rather than buying you a present for your birthday, merely sent you a check instead? Those checks were nice — in fact, when you were in college, they meant a lot — but as you got older, you probably came to realize that writing a check didn't really take all that much thought or energy.

When it comes to being a check writer, there will hopefully come a time when you have the means to assist more charities than there are hours in a day. But if you are just starting out, or if you are looking to take your practice to the next level, then your goal should be to find a single, viable charity, and grow together.

While donating money is obviously worlds better than giving nothing at all, it's not a level of commitment that is going to give either you or the charity the greatest possible return. Not when you have so much more to offer.

Second Level Involvement

To take involvement a step further and raise the overall impact of that involvement, let's say you find a worthwhile charity and decide to contribute money, time, and expertise; perhaps you're going to take a role in fundraising recruitment and (just for the sake of example) arrange for your accountant to donate a few hours a week to help them organize their books.

This is what we call "second level involvement." You're giving more than money and you're offering more than just an extra set of hands. You're providing a skill or service that the nonprofit likely can't get elsewhere. If the entity has a solid reputation and is working to effect *real* change, in the process of *physically* volunteering you are also likely to meet similar-minded people as you recruit them to assist the charity. From these actions the worst things that can happen are that your service benefits the charity, you expand your company's reach, you increase your business contacts, and you enhance your brand.

Again, everybody wins.

But while second level involvement is terrific for the charity, and very good for your practice, it's still not optimal.

Third Level Involvement

Third-level involvement is where you want to be. Take your monetary contributions and the time you volunteer. Add to those the expert application of your skills as an organizer or fundraiser, the recruitment of your accountant, and the value of networking and socializing, but this time, also add your company's name to the equation as a sponsor, either for a single large event like a golf tournament, or as the key fundraiser for a growth initiative, such as the construction of a new playground. Now you have what we call "third level involvement."

Three Levels of Community Involvement

- First level: money
- Second level: money, time, and expertise
- Third level: money, time, expertise, and sponsorship

As you've just read, the breadth of third-level involvement means that every interested party realizes the greatest benefit. In the eyes of your community you are now synonymous with change, progress, benevolence, and charity. And make no mistake, while there's absolutely no amount of involvement that can (or should) protect you from a serious legal or professional indiscretion, by publicly helping others you have earned the benefit of the doubt in our quick-to-pass-judgment culture. Simply, you are taking the steps necessary to make your firm less permeable to free-floating criticism at the same time you are helping to better the lives of the people in your community.

Not bad.

Of course, if your firm has just recently been founded, you probably won't begin your involvement at the third level; but don't sell the possibilities short, either. The beauty of third-level involvement is that your *least* important contribution is money. While a monetary donation is listed as a part of each level, the reality is that for the second and third levels, your time, expertise, and fundraising ability will take you and the charity *further* than just about any check amount you could write, especially for newer firms.

In short, we've come to understand that we help the greatest number of people when we give *of* ourselves and then *work* our way into a position of sponsorship or leadership rather than merely "buying" our way in.

Getting Started: Finding Worthwhile Charities and Projects

"Don't just give because it feels good, give because it hurts."
— Pat McClain

One of the best ways to find worthwhile charities is to ask your clients. Assisting a charity that has been referred to you by a client will enhance your existing relationship and increase loyalty.

But if a query of your clients doesn't produce a good fit, where do you go from there?

From the moment you open your doors, there'll be no shortage of charitable solicitors. But adequately vetting every request is time-consuming and problematic. And be cautious of phone solicitations, even from legitimate charities. Organizations that are using phone solicitors have usually hired a company that charges a percentage of each dollar it receives — clearly not the best way to contribute.

Organizations That Vet Charities

▪ Exempt Organizations Select Check
http://www.irs.gov/Charities-&-Non-Profits/Exempt-
Organizations-Select-Check

▪ BBB for Charities and Donors
http://necal.bbb.org/charity/

▪ Charity Navigator (Clark Howard recommended)
http://www.charitynavigator.org/

▪ CharityWatch (formerly the American Institute of Philanthropy)
http://charitywatch.org/

▪ GuideStar (lists 700,000 nonprofits and their tax-exempt status)
http://www.guidestar.org/

Websites such as these are just the entryway of the vetting process. Keep in mind that you are looking for a limited partnership
with your selected charity. You wouldn't purposely align yourself
with a criminal any more than you'd partner with someone with
no sense of what it takes to run a business. Even *unintentionally*

Pat McClain (*fifth from left*) participated in the ribbon-cutting
ceremony on January 24, 2012, for the opening of the new $3.5
million Sacramento Food Bank and Family Services education
center.

aligning yourself with an incompetent charity will damage your reputation.

In short, no matter where the referral for the charity origi-nated — a client, a neighbor, or a Magic 8 Ball — you still need to do your homework. Conduct *multiple* on-site visits where you will speak *frankly* with volunteers and employees. Then take it a step further: seek out and speak with individuals in the "target" demographic — the people the charity professes to help — and ask *if* and *how* their needs are being met. If all systems are GO — the results are positive — follow that up by heading out into the neigh-borhood. Find out if the people who live *near* the charity consider them good neighbors.

The Steps of Vetting a Charity

- Search the Internet.
- Make multiple physical visits.
- Donate something to see if the process is efficient.
- Interview employees and volunteers.
- Speak to people in the charity's specific demographic.
- Speak to people who live in the neighborhood.

Warning Signs of Combustible Charities

As with many businesses, some charities have a shelf life. They ap-pear on the scene, gain flavor-of-the-week status, and the money pours in; but then they quickly lose their effectiveness.

The very thing these two entities (for-profit and not-for-prof-it) have in common — the goal of financial stability — is often the precise thing that brings their viability to a screeching halt. Charities with excess staff and large payrolls are, just like bloated for-profit enterprises, vulnerable: vulnerable to changes in the economy, graft, greed, and excess.

It's an unfortunate glitch in human nature that some otherwise reasonable people get corrupted by access to money. They found a charity with the most honorable of intentions, but in the process, they become so successful at fulfilling their mission and procuring contributions that they begin to feel entitled and lose sight of their purpose. Again, you don't want to support or associate with charities that have lost their way. If the charity's charismatic founder is a folk hero in the community but drives a Bentley, do not turn the other cheek in deference to "all the good that he's done." Find another outlet for your involvement because that charity will crash and burn, and you may not emerge unscathed.

Location: The Closer the Better

Think local. Local charities offer you ease of access, and because you are probably going to be spending a lot of time there, the closer it is to your firm, the better. Out-of-area charities don't generally help your specific community, which is not to say that national organizations should be avoided. To the contrary, there are some great ones (the Salvation Army, Habitat for Humanity), but only become involved if they have a local presence.

Private Sector Management

Our experience has been that veterans of the *private sector* often run some of the best charities. One of the reasons is that they were trained in the management of lean-running enterprises with specific goals and short deadlines. But no matter who's in charge, *make certain they have a written mission statement with a clearly defined message* that doesn't include "Clothing the entire world in hemp by next Friday." Over-reaching charities, like government agencies, might have perfectly fine intentions, but they may be led by unrealistic dreamers who have trouble focusing on the minutia that is required to efficiently get things done.

Below are the mission statements of three charities currently rated *A* by CharityWatch.

The Hunger Project
To end hunger and poverty by pioneering sustainable, grassroots, women-centered strategies and advocating for their widespread adoption in countries throughout the world.

Reading Is Fundamental
To motivate young children to read by working with them, their parents, and community members to make reading a fun and beneficial part of everyday life. RIF's highest priority is reaching underserved children from birth to age 8.

Cancer Research Institute
Extend the lives of cancer patients and reduce cancer-related deaths by fueling the development of a new class of smarter, more effective treatments that mobilize our body's natural immune defenses against all types of cancer.

Mixing Causes

Lastly, no matter which charity or charities you choose, make certain the principals and the overall focus are aligned with both your personal and professional sensibilities. It's just good business (and good sense) to appeal to the largest possible pool in your chosen client demographic. On a personal level, having political, spiritual, or religious beliefs is admirable, but appearing militant or unyielding is not. If the charity you choose openly supports something controversial or political, you're risking a backlash. Be pragmatic. You're getting involved to help your community, not pass laws or support organizations that may upset 50% of your client base. Your first goal is to help others and your second goal is to become more visible in the community. Clients or prospective clients who see clear philosophical, spiritual, or political differences between you and them *might* suddenly choose to become ex-clients, and you may never even know why. Select charities with a clear message that, even at a glance, everyone can support and admire.

What to Look For in Your Charity

- Client recommended
- Locally based (national only if they have a local chapter)
- Tax-exempt
- Clearly defined goals and a mission statement
- A reputation that is beyond reproach
- On the move, with staff and volunteers who genuinely care about their work
- Organized with a business mindset
- Non-political
- Receptive to help

Kick-Starting Community Involvement

"A life is not important except in the impact it has on others."
— Jackie Robinson, American baseball player

While you want to begin your community involvement as soon as possible, you never want to rush into a bad fit. Understandably, most charities are hungry for assistance and when you, a financial expert with strong community ties, show up at their door, they should be welcoming.

Be quick, but don't hurry. Choose wisely and for the long haul. If you simply can't find the right fit for yourself or your practice, don't compromise; here are a couple of other options that will kick-start involvement.

Museums

Regardless of size, most cities view it as their mission to support the arts. While for-profit museums are becoming more common, many of them feature risqué installations or focus on hyper-specific target demographics that may not align with your target demographics. A majority of traditional museums remain not-for-profit and are dependent on well-connected, savvy patrons to quarterback their fundraising and growth initiatives. While dedicating yourself to a museum doesn't *precisely* meet the altruistic standards of grassroots charitable involvement, in any advisor's life there should be room for both. Besides, lots of people believe that well-run museums are essential to the enrichment of society. We agree.

For the reasons listed throughout this section, we encourage community involvement that seeks to directly help the individual. However, it's difficult to argue with the advantages that donating your energy and expertise to an established entity like a museum will present to your practice. Additionally, if you've had difficulty locating an ideal charitable entity, a museum board is a great place to begin. Your future co-board members will certainly have projects and connections that will lead to third-level involvement.

From New York City's Metropolitan Museum of Art to the Science Center of Des Moines, Iowa, a simple phone call gets the ball rolling. Almost every museum has an entire department dedicated to making it easy for people like you to get involved. Identify the museum, locate its website, and then make the call.

Libraries

What's not to love about libraries? In spite of endless predictions of their imminent demise, they've not only continued to thrive, many cities have redoubled their efforts to build new ones.

According to the American Library Association, over the past five years some cities, such as Seattle, have actually seen a 50%

increase in library patronage. As libraries have modernized and digitalized, their services have been augmented by e-book loans and free access to the Internet. Libraries have books, art, original manuscripts, antiques, film collections, computers, and historical archives. They host events of every kind and caliber, and represent, in many cities, the very heart of the cultural and fundraising community.

All of this requires money, organization, and event promotion of the highest order.

Unlike private museums, private libraries are often well-respected, and our experience with them has been excellent. They are typically supported by endowments which are augmented by private funding. In short, there is ample opportunity to simultaneously serve your community and build your practice. The people who fundraise for libraries typically come from the same socially conscious demographic as museums, with one important distinction: many libraries cater to children, which will exponentially increase the number of opportunities for you to get involved and have an impact.

How Community Involvement Benefits Your Employees

"A thread of purpose should run through our lives so that something of significance will link the years together."
— Stanley J. Weyman

While there is often some basic conflict between employer and employee, the modern, employee-friendly business model has helped to close that chasm. According to numerous studies, companies that are active in the community are more likely to attract and retain top talent. Additionally, companies that encourage their employees to participate in community involvement have significantly higher employee satisfaction levels than companies with no such philosophy.

We've covered the value of involvement to both the community and to your practice. When it comes to volunteering, much of what holds true for charity and benefactor is also true for employees. While there are more benefits for your staff than can easily be listed here, here are a few.

- Volunteerism strengthens employee identification with your firm.

- It improves employee morale.

- It helps meet professional and emotional needs that work may not satisfy.

- It broadens horizons by providing unique experiences.

- It bonds employees together, making them a stronger team.

Although you want your employees to love your company, in spite of your best efforts, not everyone will. First and foremost, no matter the job, the obligations inherent in being an "employee" preclude some personality types from viewing work as anything except a form of indentured servitude.

One of the best ways to keep employees connected and to increase enthusiasm is to involve them in projects that are larger than themselves. This is what community involvement does: It

COMMUNITY INVOLVEMENT & EMPLOYEE ENGAGEMENT

The chart at left shows the results of a study examining the effect of corporate citizenship on employee engagement. The results, which are statistically significant, show the mean engagement scores measured on a five-point scale.

Source: Northwestern University School of Education and Social Policy

improves the total work experience and makes your company matter beyond a wage or salary. When you get your company involved, your goal should be to bring your employees right along with you.

There are many ways to do this, but the best may be to actually volunteer your employees to work in the charity you've chosen. Do this by asking employees if they are interested. (They will be.) If they don't jump at the opportunity, this is one of those times when, frankly, you know best. Visit the charity *with* the employee *during business hours*, explain the mission, and ask if they'd like to spend a few hours a week helping out a worthy cause. They should find that volunteering is akin to having an entirely new job, only with none of the pressure. They'll see themselves, their work, and the world around them in a new light, and we can almost guarantee that employees will come to you refreshed and appreciative for the opportunity *you've* provided. In a sense, you are loaning out (always with the employee's consent) an employee to help the charity, which strengthens the bond between your firm, the charity, and the employee.

In-Office Involvement

"No act of kindness, no matter how small, is ever wasted."
— Aesop

In spite of all we've written, it's possible you may still want to begin your community involvement on a small scale. This sentiment is understandable; you're working to build your practice and time is at a premium.

There are literally hundreds of events you can sponsor *at the office* which will increase both morale and unity and also set the stage for larger contributions of time, money, and expertise at a later date.

Again, we urge you to get involved in your community by going out *into* the community, but there are several things you can do right from your office that will make a difference.

Small-Scale Involvement at the Office

- Blood drives (the donation truck will come right to your door)
- Toys for Tots collections
- Canned food drives
- Raising money for Guide Dogs of America
- Adopting a highway or park

While there is no wrong way to contribute to a properly vetted charity, we encourage you to start larger and then fill in the cracks with smaller efforts like those listed above. We say this because just about *any* business could host a blood drive (and you should). But when you couple the marketing limitations of our industry with your unique financial experience — which presents added value to even large charities, while simultaneously providing you with the opportunity to have the greatest impact in the shortest amount of time — the best approach for your involvement should be clear.

Going It Alone

"Be ashamed to die until you have won some victory for humanity."
— Horace Mann

The charity world does an extraordinary amount of good, but choosing one means working within an existing framework. This means partnering with entrenched principals who may or may not be open to *your* ideas.

So what other options do you have?

As a businessperson, you *could* found your own charity. But while that initiative is admirable, founding your own charity — especially early in the development of your practice — creates a level of responsibility that will rival the commitment you need to run your practice. Simply, if you can't afford to spend at least half your time running a charity you probably aren't in a position to create one.

With that in mind, there is another avenue to community involvement, one where you expand your brand, remain *in control*, and the charity of your choosing *both* supports your efforts *and* reaps terrific benefits.

Creating Your Own Event

"The only limits are, as always, those of vision."
— *James Broughton, poet*

Think big.

Fun runs, walkathons, concerts, auctions, dinner fundraisers, weekend volleyball tournaments — the possibilities for fundraising and increasing brand awareness are endless. But we are going to suggest that you start off with the near-perfect fundraiser: the golf tournament.

There are entire books dedicated to the perils of establishing your own golf tournament, but that's partly because of their popularity. To be fair, some of the concerns are justified: the headaches, the fickle sponsors, the possibility for inclement weather, people missing out on the big-picture purpose. But in our opinion, so long as you take the time to adequately prepare, golf tournaments have little downside.

Just as you created a business plan when you began your practice, we recommend you create a *written* plan for your tournament.

It doesn't have to be complicated. Every study shows that, whether writing a book, starting a business, going on a diet, or hosting a charity golf tournament, having a written plan or outline greatly streamlines the process and enhances the final product.

Basics of Charity Golf Tournaments

Volunteers

Besides your staff, if you have one, you'll need to solicit volunteers and ideas from both the golf course personnel and the charity you select as your event's beneficiary. Two things to remember: First, you are going to need more people than you realize. Better ten volunteers too many than even one too few. Second, from the moment you decide to create your tournament, you will need to *consistently* remind all involved parties what the event is for: charity. Consistent referencing of the big picture helps maintain morale while simultaneously keeping renegade egos in check.

Selecting a Charity

The charity should be local. There are several reasons for this, but its primary importance is because you are relying on local dollars and local volunteers. Ideally, the chosen charity will be capable of playing an expansive role in the execution and pro-motion of the event.

Lead Time

Eighteen months to two years. You're looking to not *only* raise serious money but *also* establish a tradition in your community. Remember, corporations tie up their charitable dollars well before the first of each year, which means you want to start recruiting them six months to a year *before* they're ready to choose their beneficiaries and sponsorship partners. And while, with hard work and diligence, you might locate donations of equipment, time, and money right up until the last minute, you want to give yourself at least six months to get everything in place and then use the remaining time to shore up and increase support. Set the foundation, get the specifics in place, and then add amenities.

Course Selection

Choose the area's best available course. A half-day tournament has the potential to attract media attention, and many otherwise private clubs that don't typically have access for non-members will be available. The ability to play on a new course gets area golfers excited, and many private courses love the exposure. You are going to want to hold your event on a weekday and select a course with the following amenities:

- Banquet facilities (complete with kitchen and sound system)
- Experienced community liaison and support staff
- Proximity to a metropolitan area
- Local hotel accommodations

If at all possible, choose a course that has hosted PGA, LPGA, or USGA events. This level of facility is always kept in premium shape and should already employ professional community relations people with existing media contacts.

Participants

Choose quality over quantity. We recommend hosting a shot-gun tournament where 18 foursomes tee off simultaneously; this means 72 participants taking over an entire golf course for around five hours. Hopefully, as you grow, you'll quickly have more than just 18 foursomes. Once you have more than 72 players, just begin to double up on foursomes on each hole with an A group and then a B group. We wouldn't recommend getting any bigger than 36 foursomes (two foursomes per hole for a total of 144 players) in any one tournament, however.

One of the bigger decisions you'll need to make is whether to include local celebrity personalities in your tournament. While television personalities, musicians, politicians, the chief of police, radio DJs, or even golf pros all add an additional level of visibility, we've been involved with large, *highly successful* events where the only names were the sponsors and the charity. Depending on the community, there may well be ample money and support available for an *entirely* businessperson-centric event. The upside to going strictly business is that you should have fewer headaches and egos than you would with a celebrity-driven tournament. Consider saving the celebrity involvement for when your event is a well-oiled and proven fundraising machine.

Awards and Prizes

Awards for participants are great. Gift bags, equipment, and gift cards are deemed sweeter when earned or won, especially in the name of charity. A $500 first prize adds a nice touch of competition to the event (and sets you up for bigger awards in the future). Most of all, however, awards and prizes (and food) give people a reason to stick around *after* the golf is complete.

Press

While getting publicity for a charity event depends on your location, it's not as difficult as it sounds. It's all about starting early. First, if you've watched (or listened to) the news recently, you've probably noticed that nearly 50% of each broadcast is devoted to human-interest stories. Between morning shows and afternoon, evening, and late-night news broadcasts, stations have a tremendous amount of airtime to fill. They love sending a camera crew out to take pictures and conduct interviews of worthwhile charity events.

If your community has no golf course with existing media contacts, and your charity is new, or small, and has never before participated in this type of endeavor, then you may find yourself recruiting media on your own. Perseverance is the key. Even local news anchors and columnists now have public email addresses. If you begin early and emphasize the charity, you should get results. The advantage is that you're selling community. Start early and stay after them.

Mission Statement

Finally, as you'd expect from a charity to which you are looking to volunteer, you want to create a simple mission statement that supports the ideals and aims of your event. Your mission statement should be devoid of catchy jargon or rhetoric. This statement is meant to lay bare your intentions in the simplest possible terms so you can economically distribute your message.

Your mission statement:

- Helps clarify and simplify your message
- Keeps you and your volunteers focused
- Motivates and galvanizes donors and participants
- Prioritizes goals
- Should be easy to remember and recite

Sample Charity Golf Tournament Mission Statement

"It is our mission to host a superb golf tournament that raises the most possible money to support The Urban Food Bank in its quest to feed our region's hungry."

The event. The goal. The charity. Everything is there. If you're like us, just reading that statement focuses your mind and excites you about the possibilities.

Is community service just dressed-up marketing?

Get involved. When you donate your energy and acumen to a charity that seeks to feed 2,000 people each week and house, clothe, and educate still hundreds more (*and then succeeds*), you can afford to let others worry about your motivations. People who are involved in their community will never criticize you for being involved in yours.

"There is no limit to what can be accomplished if it doesn't matter who gets the credit."

— Ralph Waldo Emerson

Lastly, what we often hear and what we occasionally catch ourselves thinking is "I don't have the time." Our experience has been that the first step is the most difficult, but then, naturally, the "time" finds you. It is *making* the decision to contribute that is the difference maker. The charity, your community, your firm, your brand, and your employees — all benefit when you get involved. With that in mind, we stand by our earlier pronouncement that community involvement is, for everybody, the perfect avocation.

SECTION 3
Niche Marketing

"Very narrow areas of expertise can be very productive. Develop your own profile. Develop your own niche."

— Leigh Steinberg

Niche: *a position particularly well suited to the person who occupies it*

Niche Market: *the subset of the market on which a specific product or service is focused*

Niche Marketing: *Concentrated marketing efforts on a specific and well-defined market segment.*

Aim Small, Miss Small (And Still Hit Your Target)

While marketing is integral to your success, it's actually a general term that encompasses various practices intended to enhance your brand and build your business by both directly and indirectly attracting and then keeping clients. It encompasses advertising, branding, customer satisfaction, and much more.

Niche marketing, on the other hand, is where the focus gets narrow.

In the investment advisory sector, niche marketing is the process by which you work to position yourself to meet the needs of a particular subsection of the general market. The niche can be a group, collection, organization, or an association comprised of people who have something significant in common that makes some aspect of their advisory needs similar, so that a specific marketing (and advising) approach appeals to most or even every member of the segment.

How specific you need to get to find a true niche depends on your market. But if the individuals and assets are present (or, in the case of assets, will *eventually* be present), an opportunity to cultivate a niche market may exist.

The Narrowcast Mindset

It would be next to impossible for us to present a section about niche markets without telling our specific story. That's because early on in our careers we identified a target demographic, but we developed the processes through trial and error, and only then as we moved forward. Above all else, we were persistent, and that persistence led to the development of processes which we honed over time. What follows are the best practices gleaned from those years of trial and error, and the foundation of the model we both use *and teach* now.

When we first identified our preferred niche market some 20 years ago, it had two of the most important variables for success: It was all around us, meaning it had large numbers of potential clients, but it also had very substantial barriers to entry, which are the obstacles that keep other advisors from penetrating or even pursuing the market. So, while it's true that over the years our *general* marketing efforts have become significantly broader, it's also true that we built Hanson McClain Advisors on a niche market that, in part, we pioneered.

Many advisors see niche marketing as merely identifying a subsection of the population and then positioning oneself to cultivate it more aggressively than they pursue the general market. Technically, that's accurate. The subsection "widows of orthopedic surgeons" is technically a niche market, but it lacks a true barrier to entry. For our purposes, we want to explore the search more deeply.

For a niche market, you're searching for something more than merely any individual with x number of assets. *Every* advisor wants those clients so the competition is fierce. You're looking for a segment that is receptive to a tailored marketing and advising approach that both educates *and meets the needs* of the individuals therein. You're also searching for something that has either been underserved or remains unidentified.

Advantage of a Niche Market Focus

"Perhaps the single biggest question any potential client has is: 'What can YOU offer me that no one else can?'"
— Scott Hanson

It's pretty straightforward: You don't hire a tennis coach to teach you how to act, and rare are the clients who will hire an advisor who doesn't understand what's unique or complex about their specific goals or financial situation. To widen the net, the deeper your insights and knowledge of a group's needs, the more likely you are to be selected to advise members of the market.

While it's difficult to position yourself as a general practitioner and then still thrive as an investment advisor, this is especially true if you are just starting out. That's because a major aspect of client accumulation involves trust: the trust that you will serve their best interests and the trust that you do indeed know what you're doing. Rookies can't just borrow a track record. Trust takes time to build. So if you don't already operate a firm with 20 years of investment advisory history and neck-high referrals, or if you have a mature firm that has stagnated, we suggest you consider recalibrating and adopting a niche model.

So what are some of the primary advantages of focusing on a niche market?

- A clearly defined market strategy, aimed at a specific demographic, allows you to create and perfect a more compelling message than a competitor who is positioned as a general practitioner.

- You are on the inside, while your competition is forced to wait outside the door.

- You're potentially developing an ongoing pipeline of new clients that could continue throughout your entire career.

You are in competition with other advisors. In a general market, it's a good bet that for every available client, you have numerous competitors who are minor experts in just about any subset — not to be confused with niche market — of the population (i.e., they can boast of the experience of having worked with trial attorneys with two ex-wives because two of their clients fit that description).

Having a target-specific practice is not *only* one of the best ways to build your firm, but being an expert in your target niche will benefit your clients, whose financial needs you'll be expertly addressing. So whether you refer to it as niche marketing, niche-mining, niche-pioneering, targeting, or specialization, one of the best ways to grow your practice is by directing your acquisition strategy, *and your advising focus*, squarely at a viable niche (or, depending on your geography, *possibly* two or three). This means finding a niche that:

- Is a true subsegment of the general market (or the pre-general market, if their assets are currently unavailable)

- Shares common needs and interests (i.e., members of a company or industry with a dedicated pension or defined contribution plan)

- Is reasonably plentiful (a large company, or an entire sector of an industry that is specific to your region or otherwise geographically desirable)

- Is largely ignored by the competition, ideally because it has barriers to entry

Again, if you become an expert in the needs that are specific to the niche, you're positioning yourself as *the* option when those clients are ready to work with an advisor.

Identifying a New or Narrow Market with Barriers to Entry

When we founded Hanson McClain Advisors, we went all in on our chosen niche. It was one of the best decisions we ever made.

We were in our 20s and just starting out — we hardly had any capital — and yet we went out and selected a niche that actually offered us only a limited opportunity to immediately manage client assets.

Choosing to work with this niche meant delaying gratification.

Poor cash flow probably *should* have sent us in search of every type of client we could identify, but we didn't stray from our plan. Instead, we saw the future opportunities that existed, and so we took the long view and doggedly pursued our target niche, which was a good-sized entity that had been largely underserved if not entirely ignored.

Most advisors believe there are but two main ways to acquire clients: Either be there when the money is in transition, say after an inheritance or when a person retires, or be there because the client is unhappy with their current advisor and prepared to make a change. Being that we were young and had relatively little experience, and being that we were determined in spite of our youth to be independent investment advisors and go it alone, we knew that we'd have a hard time wooing retirement-ready investors or the wealthy, who were typically more than twice our age. Determined to find a third way, we dedicated ourselves to pursuing the Northern California employees of AT&T.

While AT&T is a world-famous company with tens of thousands of employees *nationwide,* locally, the barrier to entry for advisors was that the members of this niche were not only still employed but also not particularly well paid, by the manageable-assets rating standards of most investment advisors.

So why go after this demographic when they had yet to retire and they had no money to invest?

Once we researched the data, we knew we had an opportunity. The reason is that AT&T not only sponsors defined benefit plans (pensions) for their employees, they also sponsor defined contribution plans (401(k)s). By modern business standards, where pensions are rarely offered to new hires, AT&T's retirement plans, even for service technicians, operators, and linesmen, approach the gold standard by paralleling the modern public sector retirement plan model.

There are *thousands* of AT&T employees just in the Sacramento region. Our research revealed that upon retirement, and in lieu of a monthly pension, most usually elected to receive a $300,000 to $400,000 lump-sum payout, in addition to whatever they'd accrued in their 401(k) plans. This meant that some of these employees would have accumulated over $700,000 by the time they retired, and they would also *still* have Social Security to rely on.

We took to calling this demographic the "mass affluent." As just about any lottery winner will tell you, people who have earned $50,000 a year over the course of their careers are rarely prepared to properly manage a $700,000 lump sum that comes their way. We knew they'd need assistance managing those assets. And we wondered, *What would it take to become AT&T's go-to advisory firm for the Sacramento region?*

Realizing we needed to get inside the company, we dedicated ourselves to:

- Becoming experts in the AT&T retirement and pension plans
- Educating those employees about their retirement plans
- Establishing relationships that would be mutually beneficial over an extended duration of time

Eighteen months after we first created our marketing plan to capture the AT&T market, we became so well-known to their employees that we were sometimes given unoccupied offices to work in whenever we visited their facilities.

So how did we accomplish this? On the back end, after we got through the door, was the hard work of gaining knowledge, marketing, promoting, hosting workshops, and building a database, which we'll cover in a moment. But out front were the barriers to entry. Great niches may have several barriers. Think of it as the perfect gift wrapped up in numerous ribbons and layers of paper. While not having money to immediately invest was the main barrier to entry which had kept most other advisors from cultivating the preretirement employees at AT&T, it certainly wasn't the only one.

Below is a list of barriers to entry that we identified as we built up our relationship with AT&T. This list has dual purposes: Besides enumerating many of the barriers to entry to AT&T, it also represents many of the exact things you should *actually consider looking for* to help you identify a worthwhile niche market:

- Workers who are still employed
- Middle income (or they would already be targeted)
- A large company, the bigger the better
- Good retirement plans, with pensions and/or 401(k)s and company stock

- Secure offices and facilities (fences keep out other advisors, but not you)
- Unionized
- Has some need that is not being met (perhaps no one understands their retirement plan)
- No track record of previous cultivation by advisors (niche members are unfamiliar with the advantages of receiving professional investment and planning advice or working with advisors)
- A major company in transition, if not outright upheaval (large companies in transition often offer thousands of simultaneous early retirement buyouts; employees concerned for their futures need professional financial advice)
- A general suspicion of outsiders (once you're inside, this works to your advantage)

Remember, barriers to entry give you an edge. While seemingly a nuisance, they are the very reason that the untapped niche exists. The niche, at a glance, is thought to be too difficult to break into. But barriers exist in all worthwhile niches. They work in your favor by keeping others out.

Marketing to the Niche

"The aim of marketing is to know and understand the customer so well the product or service fits him and sells itself."
— Peter F. Drucker

As presented in the first section of this book, the first thing you should do is develop a marketing plan that is specific to your niche. According to a 2009 Wharton School study, only 38% of companies have an updated plan, and yet it only takes an hour or so to create a tool that can help guide you to your destination. It need only be a page or two long, but it's vital. In fact, at the risk of being redundant, marketing plans are the one thing all great marketers agree on: You need one. Create it today.

Once complete, *read over the plan each morning* to help refocus your mind. (Use the marketing plan in the first section of this book as your guide.)

Our success with the AT&T market didn't occur overnight. In the beginning, we were on the outside looking in. No one on the inside or in HR was asking us to come over and present our services. We needed an ice breaker, an introduction, so the first thing we did was create a workshop flyer and then stand outside the facility greeting each arriving and departing employee.

Getting doors to open need not be any more sophisticated than that. When we showed up the following week to introduce ourselves in person, people thanked us and gave us a few moments of their time.

We were on our way.

Remember, it's simply not enough to occasionally stop by your niche target's work area, if they are all or even mostly in one location, and introduce yourself at the gate and perhaps hand out business cards. But it's a start. Cultivating a niche and then cornering a market takes innovation and a focused, long-term approach. The initial contact can come from just about anything.

A few examples would be:

- Deliver ice cream or pizza with your company's mission statement attached. Inexpensive, large banners with your company's name can be draped on the truck.

- Check your database for "ins." You might already have a client who worked for the company before retiring.

- Ask neighbors, friends, or relatives if they have any contacts in the company.

- Call the company. *Ask* how you can gain access.

- Call the head of HR and ask him or her out to lunch.
- Identify the union leader and ask him or her out to lunch.
- Find the yard or office and see where they like to go after work.

Market niches grow their own tentacles. Our success with AT&T, and afterward with telecom and utility company employees in our own region, was just the beginning of our niche market story. In 1998, just five years after founding Hanson McClain Advisors, our AT&T penetration had drawn so much attention and become so successful that independent investment advisors from around the country began to contact us about the possibility of our training them. Be it the regional power company or an oil company giant with local offices and plants, the advisors had identified the niches and they wanted to know how to get inside.

In response to this need, we created the Hanson McClain Retirement Network, which has contracted with some 200-plus advisors from around the country and provided support and training in exchange for a percentage of assets won from telecom and utility company employees. In the more than 15 years since the founding of the HMRN, we've assisted partner-advisors in the accumulation of almost $4 billion in assets under advisement. Our niche marketing strategy has been used

by advisors from around the country to work with pre-retirees from companies such as Chevron, Southwestern Bell, Southern California Edison, Southern California Gas Company, Duke Energy, Nevada Power Company, Alabama Power, Pacific Bell, PG&E, and many others.

The Multi-Pronged Marketing Approach

As we began to make contacts inside AT&T, we quickly realized the potential was there: The company had many older employees with regular buyout offers and lots of confusion about the specifics of the company's retirement plans. As often happens in large companies, rules related to retirement and benefits were changing all the time, and there was a lot of confusion among AT&T's employees. Our goal, and yours, is to provide a service, which in a scenario such as this one is initially going to focus on education. You will probably find, as we did, that most of the employees in your niche have never spoken to an investment advisor in their life.

Once in the door, then what do you do? Upon breaching the niche market wall, you should immediately:

- Subscribe to all publications relevant to the niche. Information is your partner.

- Join the union (or any related club or organization).

- Attend company meetings that focus on retirement. (You'll typically be completely welcome.)

Information on retirement plans is actually fairly easy to locate. Most unions post them online, or employees will provide them for you. Remember, *they want help.* Once you establish trust and expertise, they'll be on your side. There is never any reason to mislead or be duplicitous. If you believe complete honesty won't succeed, then the niche isn't for you — or maybe *you* aren't for the niche. You are there to provide a service that the employees can choose to utilize, or not. Large majorities of the people we come into contact with from our niche understand this and appreciate that our aim is to provide them with a service that will help them achieve their goals. We are meeting a need. And with the sometimes acrimonious nature of the employer-employee relationship, especially in larger companies, our experience has been that the employees appreciate having someone knowledgeable on their side.

So, your overarching initial goals should be to:

- Identify the niche.
- Find a way inside.
- Join the club.
- Become an expert in their specific retirement plans.

Conducting Workshops

Once you've gained a foothold, it's time to take it up a notch. As much as anything we do within our niche, workshops have been *the* vital component in transitioning people from being prospective clients into clients. We can repeat that last sentence in all capital letters if it will help. WORKSHOPS ARE WHERE IT'S AT.

Here's the entire process of preparing for and then executing employee education workshops:

Step One: *Dates, Locations, and Menu*

Before the first of every year, decide how many workshops you are going to sponsor. Because AT&T has such a presence in the Sacramento region, we typically conduct three workshops for their employees each quarter, usually holding them in three different parts of the city over the course of the same week. Once we pick the dates, say, the first week of April, we then select the locations. We've been working with the same restaurants for many years, but you need to establish not only primary relationships but backup locations as well. Your preferred venue may not be available when you need it.

What you want in a location depends on who comprises your niche. We like to serve dinner at our workshops, and we always invite attendees to bring their spouses, so we've found that the ideal location is a steakhouse with a private room. You are treating them to dinner and educating them on a topic that is important, so you want them to have a good meal, but you are also building rapport and acquiring information. Comfort and convenience are the keys.

After we reserve the restaurants, we set about creating the menu. You want to emphasize to the restaurant that this will

Hanson McClain

SMART PLANNING IN THE NEW PENSION ERA

Retirement workshops for **AT&T Management Employees**

- When is the **best time** for me to **retire**?
- How do I **avoid** a **10% early withdraw penalty**?
- How does the 4 year **PPA** phase-in affect **my Lump Sum**?
- How do I receive the **IPRO®** - the personal retirement plan designed exclusively for **telecommunications employees**?

FREE *educational workshops. Dinner will be served!*

Tuesday, June 18th 6:00 PM	Cattlemen's 2000 Taylor Road – Roseville, CA
Thursday, June 20th 6:00 PM	Zinfandel Grille 2384 Fair Oaks Boulevard – Sacramento, CA
Wednesday, June 26th 6:00 PM	Cattlemen's 12409 Folsom Boulevard – Rancho Cordova, CA

Reservations required as seating is limited. RSVP Today!
Call (916) 979-4077 or (888) 979-4077
Hanson McClain and Hanson McClain Advisors are
independent entities neither endorsed, affiliated nor retained by AT&T.
Please note that CWA does not recommend or sponsor any individual or outside organization.
CWA members assume full responsibility for their financial decisions. 3/13

Hanson McClain®
Independent and Proud of It

800·482·2196 | *HansonMcClain.com*

SECURITIES OFFERED THROUGH
HANSON MCCLAIN
A REGISTERED BROKER/DEALER
MEMBER FINRA/SIPC.

ADVISORY SERVICES OFFERED
THROUGH HANSON MCCLAIN
ADVISORS.

A example of the flyer Hanson McClain uses to promote workshops.

be a regularly scheduled event so that the staff and restaurant manager will be more likely to do the little things that make the evening special. We typically tell the restaurant that we'd like three to five choices for dinner, and then we work out a set price for each attendee. (Because of the volume discount, it's usually under $20 per person.)

Attendees typically order their dinner choice just as they arrive.

Step Two: *The Flyer*

Six weeks before the first workshop, we create the flyer. The flyer design changes each year, and is updated based on workshop location and date. The flyer is used in several different steps of the process, which we'll illustrate below.

Step Three: *The Direct Mailer*

Four weeks prior to any series of workshops, we put together a mailer. If you're just starting out and your database is still thin, utilize any contacts you have at the company to accumulate names. (More on building your niche database coming up.) We send the mailer to three categories of AT&T employees from our database, which we have ranked based on time of service, not assets. The three ranks are:

1. **Status Zero:** 30 years of service. Eligible to retire at any time, regardless of age.

2. **Status One:** Pension eligible, but with age discounts (29 years or less of service, under the age of 55).

3. **Status Two:** Within five years of pension eligibility.

To repeat, unlike the way we rank our general marketing clients, we don't rank AT&T employees (whom we call *prospec*tive clients) based on assets. The only thing we are concerned with is retirement eligibility. We want to know *when* they are eligible to become clients. (We also have a Status Three in our database, which includes employees who are more than five years away from retirement.)

\<Date\>

\<First name\> \<Last name\>
\<Address\>
\<City\>, \<State\>, \<Zip\>

Dear \<Insert First name\>,

In 2013, the PPA interest rate phase-in will be at 50%. Are you comfortable with how this formula will impact your pension? As an **independent** financial advisory firm that has in-depth knowledge of your employer's retirement plans, we would like to invite you to attend a complimentary workshop that will help you better understand your options.

At *Hanson McClain* we have helped literally thousands of telecommunications employees from across the nation transition into retirement. One of the ways we do this is by educating employees so that they can make informed decisions about their company pension plan.

Enclosed are two flyers that highlight our next workshop: *SMART PLANNING IN THE NEW PENSION ERA.* Keep one flyer for yourself, and please consider taking the other one to work to give to a colleague.

To learn more about *Hanson McClain*, an **independent** financial advisory firm, you can visit us online at www.HansonMcClain.com or call us at (888) 979-4077.

We look forward to seeing you at the *SMART PLANNING IN THE NEW PENSION ERA* workshop!

Regards,

Your Team at Hanson McClain

P.S. Tune in to our Money Matters call-in radio program on 1530AM KFBK, Saturdays from 10:00-11:00am with a rebroadcast Sundays from 2:00-3:00pm.

Hanson McClain and Hanson McClain Advisors are independent entities neither endorsed, affiliated nor retained by AT&T. 05/13

The direct mail letter Hanson McClain sends to prospective workshop attendees.

In the mailer we include a letter, two event flyers, and on the back of one of the flyers is something we call the PIRF.

The Pension Information Request Form for contacts is probably the most important form in the packet. The PIRF is used to create our database, and not only do we recommend sending it with the mailer, we *highly* recommend you create a version that suits your needs, and carry it with you whenever you might come into contact with individuals from your niche.

Pension Information Request

Mail or fax to the address or number below:
Hanson McClain
3620 Fair Oaks Blvd, Suite 300
Sacramento, CA 95864
Telephone: (916) 979-4077 or (888) 979-4077
Fax: (916) 483-9661
www.HansonMcClain.com

Employee Name

Date of Birth (mm/dd/yy)

Spouse Name

Home Address

Home Phone

City   Zip Code

Personal Email Address

Employee Information

Job Title

Work Phone

NCS Date (mm/dd/yy)

Mobile/Pager #

Work Address   Room#

Fax #

City   Zip

This copy is for your friend,
so they too may receive
important pension information!

How We Can Help!

✓ **FREE** retirement consultations for all AT&T employees
✓ **FREE** educational workshops on AT&T's Pension and Company Savings Plans
✓ Assists AT&T employees plan their retirement with the
Independent Personal Retirement Overview (IPRO®)

Hanson McClain has assisted thousands of AT&T employees with their retirement.

HM Hanson McClain·
Independent Investment Advice

Hanson McClain and Hanson McClain Advisors are independent entities neither endorsed,
affiliated nor retained by AT&T. CWA does not recommend or sponsor any individual or outside organization. CWA members assume full
responsibility for their financial decisions. 01/11

The pension information request form, or PIRF.

Step Four: *Email Blast*

The PIRF (or your comparable form) helps you accumulate email addresses. Two weeks before the event, we send out an email blast invitation to all Status Zero, Status One, and Status Two employees in our database.

Step Five: *Event Promotion*

One week prior to the first workshop of each series, we go out to the AT&T offices and maintenance yards and promote the workshops for two or three full days. We usually make 6–10 stops each day. We take flyers and hand them out, pin them to boards, leave them at the front desk, and so on.

After the physical promotion, we usually have an estimate of the number of attendees. We call the restaurant and give them a

---

Subject: You're Invited – AT&T Pension Workshop – RSVP Today!

Hanson McClain Advisors invites you to join us for a free retirement workshop titled **"SMART PLANNING IN THE NEW PENSION ERA."** This workshop is specifically designed for AT&T management employees. Seating is limited! ***RSVP today*** for this free educational workshop at 888.979.4077 or <u>Register Online</u>. Topics to be covered include:

- How will the **Cam Benefit be affected** by the **PPA Rate?**
- What is **Separation from Service** and how do I use it to **avoid** the **10% Penalty?**
- Am I **prepared** for the **50% GATT** and **50% PPA** in **2013?**

Come for a complimentary dinner, courtesy of Hanson McClain, and get the answers to these questions (and many more) at one of these **FREE** educational workshops!

- **Tuesday, June 18th at 6:00 PM**
  - ○ Cattlemen's – 2000 Taylor Road, Roseville, CA 95678
- **Thursday, June 20th at 6:00 PM**
  - ○ Zinfandel Grille – 2384 Fair Oaks Blvd., Sacramento, CA 95825
- **Wednesday, June 26th at 6:00 PM**
  - ○ Cattlemen's – 12409 Folsom Blvd., Rancho Cordova, CA 95670

We look forward to seeing you!

Sincerely,

Your team at Hanson McClain Advisors

(To opt out of future email messages from Hanson McClain, please <u>Contact Us</u>.)

Recipients of this Sample email blast can click the words "Register Online" to go directly to our website.

head count. Over the last 20 years, the number of workshop attendees has averaged about 18 employees, not including spouses, which means the hard costs for an event are just over $700.

Step Six: *Event Materials*

For each attendee we create packets, which include a PIRF, informational handouts covering topics such as "Four Things You Should Know about Your Advisor," handouts outlining any changes to their specific retirement or pension plans, two promotional flyers for our next round of workshops, and, most importantly, the Independent Personal Retirement Overview. The IPRO is a customized four-page tool upon which we document information such as pension, savings, 401(k), other assets, debt, home equity, and more. It's a tool we've created that was several years in the making and which can be used to help calculate how much money it should take for the client to achieve their retirement goals.

Step Seven: *The Presentation*

Our presentations run just over an hour, with time set aside afterward for questions. We recommend you utilize a Power-Point presentation, but an overhead projector works fine. (Make certain you know the technical capacities of your restaurant. Do they have a video screen?) Remember, employees attend because they want to learn about their retirement plans. As we've been working with AT&T for so long and because as members of the union we receive all pertinent pension and retirement plan mail and also subscribe to every relevant document, periodical, and magazine, we pride ourselves on knowing more about AT&T's retirement plans than even their own internal HR personnel, who tend to have a large turnover.

Typically, the presentation covers the latest developments

regarding their plans and buyout offers, IRS guidelines, and what the transition to retirement will entail. For 2013, we added workshops that focus on Social Security, which have proven to be extremely popular. When you set up presentations to your niche market, you are there to add value to the experience of attendees, gain trust, and secure your position as an expert in their retirement plans.

Toward the end of the evening, we discuss the PIRF. As an inducement to encourage them to fill out a copy, we offer a pizza dinner for 20 to the person whose copy is chosen in a drawing. We get everyone to fill out a PIRF this way. A few days after the workshop, we have six or seven pizzas delivered to a destination of their choosing, sometimes to the service techs who work right in the maintenance yard.

To repeat, the pizza drawing ensures everyone has filled out a PIRF, plus we attend the pizza dinner, which gives us another chance to connect with the employees in the niche.

Independent
Personal
Retirement
Overview

The Independent Personal Retirement Overview, or IPRO, is completed at events.

Step Eight: *After the Workshop*

The morning after, the first thing you should have an associate do is to add (or crosscheck) any information from the PIRFs with your database. Focus your attention on Status Zeros, or people who are eligible to retire.

Later that day, we call all Status Zeros to schedule appointments and to follow up on any questions they may have, and if we don't hear back, we call them again the next day. If still no word, seven days later, we make another call. If we still don't connect, we call again one month after the workshop, and then every six months thereafter.

We invite all Status Zeros in for a *complimentary*, one-on-one retirement planning consultation every year, at which time we go over their IPRO and answer any questions they may have. Appointments typically last an hour.

Status Ones we invite in every 18 to 24 months, and we touch base with them at least once a year, making certain to ask, "Have there been any developments in regard to your retirement date?" Once they transition to Status Zero, we automatically step up the contacts and appointments to the level noted above.

Starting Out and Getting In the Door

"A dream doesn't become reality through magic; it takes sweat, determination and hard work."
— Colin Powell

Almost every town and region has a major company or organization that would be worth cultivating as a niche. If you can't easily identify a target off the top of your head, we have these suggestions:

- Call the local Chamber of Commerce. Ask for a list of the 30 largest companies in your region.

- Google companies in your town. You may be surprised to learn that just outside your city, in a business park you may not even know about, a company with 3,000 employees may be headquartered.

- Brainstorm with associates, neighbors, friends, and people in the groups or organizations to which you belong.

- Knock on doors. Drive up to the security booth in business parks and ask who is headquartered there.

Identifying opportunities that are just beneath the surface takes perseverance. Those barriers to entry may seem ominous and too high to scale, but they also may well crumble at the slightest touch. You're looking to provide a service. Statistics show that people who go it alone, in terms of investing, perform worse than those who seek professional guidance. Add to that the fact that you may well have expertise in insurance, estate planning,

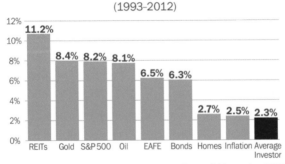

20-Year Annualized Returns by Asset Class
(1993-2012)

Source: JP Morgan, June 2013

Investors who handle their assets without professional guidance have a lower rate of return.

taxation, planning for college, and much more. Remember, no
one likes to feel like they are being sold something, but just about
everyone loves having an expert they can rely on who has their
best interests at heart.

A Few More Points to Consider: Watch Your Reputation

Niche markets tend to be very viral. That means your integrity is
of the utmost importance. You need to avoid alienating anyone
in your niche, especially if that niche is one large company to
which you've gained entry.

Embrace the Delayed Gratification

After you become an advisor you want to get cracking by marketing to and *advising* clients. We understand. We assume you're
willing to work hard and sacrifice and, above all, maintain integrity. But the discipline to delay your gratification — even just a
little — should pay off much more down the line if you're able to
identify a market that is underserved or even ignored. They exist.
It may not be a phone company, but somewhere nearby there's
probably a market waiting to be discovered.

Steady Wins the Day

Once you find your niche, don't start fast and then taper off.
You wouldn't be an advisor without the ability to follow through.
Gather motivation from the future you want to have. Trust is built
through consistent performance. *Keep* visiting and marketing to
your niche, even if everyone in the company already knows your
name. Sharks are circling, and your success will draw them in.
Keep them away by continuing to perform. More than anything,
navigating a niche takes follow-up in the form of follow-through.
People have questions that they want answered. You are the expert.
You are the answer provider. You meet needs.

Software to Manage Your Entire Niche Database

Advances in customer service software have improved our operations and efficiency, which means they have brought added value to the client experience, as well. The most important mechanism for tracking your niche market is your CRM (customer relationship management) software. None of your processes should be manual. We use Salesforce for the management of our niche market prospective client database, as well as for all of our marketing analytics (which we'll present in the next section).

We use the software Junxure as our firm's main CRM software to manage existing clients. While it has several advantages, Junxure is particularly compliance-friendly because it keeps good records, and it summons and displays client details in a format that allows advisors and assistants to easily access and view the answers they most need when they are working with clients.

Every 30 minutes, Salesforce automatically syncs with Junxure, and then Junxure automatically links to Outlook for calendaring appointments.

Identifying the CRM that best meets your needs, and making certain that everyone in your office masters it, is one of the most important components of systematizing your business and improving the client experience.

Identifying Niches Is a Mindset

Don't simply look for a large market. Find a large market with a need. In 2003, we realized that many seniors owned their own homes but were otherwise cash poor. We saw the need for reverse mortgages, so we founded Liberty Reverse Mortgage. Before it was acquired by Fortune 500 Company Genworth Financial in 2007, we grew it into the third largest reverse mortgage company in America. It's now the largest reverse mortgage company in the country.

We've already told you about the Hanson McClain Retirement Network: 15 years of niche market advisor training and still going strong.

Since the inception of the 401(k) in the 1980s, the assortment of available investment options for plan participants has been held captive by plan sponsors: 10–40 mutual funds and access to company stock.

Well-meaning as plan sponsors might be, many have little fiduciary or investment experience. But for plan participants? As noted above, while the choices for their investments have been limited, there's been almost no direct access to receive professional allocation advice.

In response to savvy savers wanting more control over their 401(k) plans, in the late 1990s sponsors began adding the Self-Directed Brokerage Account option to their assortments. Many SDBAs allow participants to work with an advisor.

Suddenly, plan participants gained a measure of control.

Yet while the SDBA option was a step forward for participants, it still largely left them to fend for themselves. In response to having more control over their allocation, many 401(k) participants utilized the SDBA option to invest emotionally in properties like gold and Apple stock.

We identified a need.

In 2012, we founded Pathway Strategic Advisors, which uses on-plan asset management to allow us to actively manage the defined contribution plan savings of our partners' clients. Through Pathway, solicitor-advisors work with us to manage the money in their clients' 401(k), 403(b) and 457 plans.

According to the Investment Company Institute, there are now roughly 60 million 401(k) accounts in America, encompassing perhaps $4 trillion in savings. Through the SDBA option and Pathway, clients can gain access to ongoing, professional money management services. And yet all of this happens *without* removing those funds from the original 401(k) platform.

Liberty Reverse Mortgage, the Hanson McClain Retirement Network, Pathway Strategic Advisors — these companies were not founded merely to be profitable; they were created in response to needs. Where needs exist, answers, opportunity, and, ideally, profit will follow.

Looking for a niche market? Remember to look for markets that are:

- Underserved or ignored
- Have large numbers of potential clients
- Has a need that is not being met
- Have barriers to entry
- Have workers who are still employed
- Have solid retirement plans (pensions or 401(k)s)

Perhaps just across the street from you is a company with employees who have a need. Niche marketing begins with the mindset that you are looking for something that may exist in plain sight but has been overlooked by the competition because of the barriers to entry.

Identify your niche, create your marketing plan, overcome those barriers, and then work to corner that market. Do this, and the general market will beat a path to your door.

SECTION 4
Assessments and Analytics
Determining Whether Your Marketing Efforts Are Successful

marketing campaign: *a coordinated series of steps that can include promotion of a product through different mediums (television, radio, print, online) using a variety of different types of advertisements, but also word of mouth (source: Investopedia)*

analytics: *the discovery and communication of meaningful patterns in data (source: Wikipedia)*

Assessments and Analytics

While the most common perception of marketing is associated with ad campaigns such as television or radio commercials, marketing also includes the compilation of client information *and* analytics.

The compilation of client information includes the screening process by which first-time callers and prospective clients are vetted against the account minimums and standards of your firm.

Marketing analytics is the knowledge gained from the analysis of the data that is collected related to a campaign, and, after that, it's how that data measuring a campaign's results and effectiveness is used to shape future marketing decisions.

In this section, Assessments and Analytics, we're going to present some of the basic processes by which we gather data on prospective clients, and then outline the methods we use to determine the effectiveness of our marketing, along with how we utilize those findings to refine our goals.

THE MARKETING ANALYSIS CYCLE

Source: The Cross Channel Conversation, May 2013

The Marketing Analysis Cycle

First, here's something to consider: almost no matter what mechanisms you have in place to appraise your marketing progress, *some* hoped-for findings may initially elude you. That's because it's difficult to *precisely* measure the impact of any *individual* campaign on long-term brand building. Things such as short-term campaign analytics and year-to-year cumulative progress are absolutely measurable and worthwhile — we would even go so far as to call them "essential." The brand tentacles that have resulted from a succession of good campaigns make any single campaign the second front of effective marketing, with important long-term repercussions, but its effects are difficult to *statistically* quantify except by appraisal of your firm's bottom line.

On the upside (which is what this section is primarily focused on), analyzing your marketing data should not only reveal insights that will provide you with a much clearer understanding of which campaigns have worked, and which have not, but also help you to better understand your business.

We have always believed that the more you understand about your business and your industry, the greater the possibility for achieving a deeper, lasting success.

Marketing Overview: Campaigns

As outlined previously, we built our business from a niche market outward. The more successful we became in our niche, the more successful we became *outside* our niche in the general market. A part of this is due to our success within the niche: A thousand clients from one entity have tens of thousands of friends, relatives, neighbors, and acquaintances who are potential clients via referral. But another part of it is that as we mastered the niche and gained a track record, we began to expand our general market advertising and outreach.

Below is a list of our various marketing campaigns:

- Quarterly mailers
- Social media
- Quarterly investment newsletters
- Intensive community involvement with title sponsorships including signage
- Weekly call-in radio program
- Radio advertising
- Magazine advertising
- Niche market workshops
- Email blasts
- Press releases
- Newspaper advertising
- Book(s) (general market release)
- Website banners
- Television advertising

As you'll read in the following pages, we've developed systems to measure various categories of effectiveness for *every* campaign on our marketing list. It is our intention that our experience should be transferrable to your business, regardless of size or budget, and help to hone and improve your specific marketing tactics.

Building Databases and First-Time Callers

We gather information for our niche markets primarily through the distribution and collection of pension information request forms, or via telephone or web inquiry. But what about first-time, general market callers to our offices?

It's of paramount importance to find out how *every* caller found you. The origin of every first-time caller needs to be recorded in your database under its own category (e.g., found us through the radio show, a magazine ad, our newsletter, a workshop, etc.).

The moment the phone rings, a marketing mechanism begins. The operator asks for the caller's name, and then immediately types it into the computer. If there's no match, the operator asks, "Are you a first-time caller to our firm?"

If the answer is in the affirmative, the operator calls the marketing department, provides the caller's name and status to our personnel, and then forwards the call.

In regard to calls, here's an important point: *Every* caller to our firm during business hours speaks to an actual person (and not voice mail). If you are just starting out and your office consists of just a couple of people, this may not always be possible. But in larger offices like our own, we utilize a phone queue system that starts with the receptionist, and if he or she is occupied, the phones on a second level begin to ring. If the call still isn't picked up within two additional rings, the circle of ringing phones extends to a third level of personnel. This way, every call to our firm is answered by an actual person and never by voice mail.

Year in and year out, we receive as many compliments about never sending a client to voice mail as just about anything else. The fact is, it matters a great deal to our clients, and so it matters to us.

The team members of our marketing department are as *specifically* trained as almost any entity at Hanson McClain Advisors. Besides the implementation of many of our marketing campaigns, they're also experts at asking sensitive questions. Much time and energy has gone into developing the various scripts so that the questions are effectively presented in a non-threatening manner.

When the call is transferred, the team member in the marketing department answers by saying, "Hello Mrs. Smith, this is (name), how may I help you today?"

We have two general market retail divisions: "Select" and "HMA." Our Select designation (which we developed as recently as 2010) is reserved for individuals whose investible assets are between $50,000 and $300,000. Our HMA clients are those with investible assets of $300,000 or more (which was increased from $250,000 in early 2013). That's two major changes to the way we categorize accounts, *and* to who exactly meets our account minimums in just three years. (As a side note, the *primary* difference between Select and HMA is the level of service provided.)

We ask first-time callers about their financial information *before* we seek their personal contact information so that if they do not meet the account minimums, or if they would prefer a different compensation model (such as "fee for service" planning) than the one we offer, we can make that distinction quickly, which respects both the caller's time and ours.

Below is a script for the information gathering of first-time callers:

First-Time General Market Prospective Clients

How can I help you today? _____

How did you hear about Hanson McClain? (Source)

_____

Can you tell me a little about your situation and the type of services you are seeking: _____

Are you currently working or retired?   Working ☐   Retired ☐

IF WORKING: Who do you currently work for?

_____

How long have you worked for your employer? _____

(We assist individuals who will be retiring in 3-5 years and have investments available to be managed upon retirement)

Are you participating in a company savings plan, such as a 401(k), 457 plan (state employees), or 403(b)?

_____

Does your employer offer a pension? _____

Does your pension have a lump sum option? _____

Can you tell me a little bit about the investments you current-ly hold? _____

☐ 401(k) (investible if within 5 years of retirement)
Approx Value _____

☐ 403(b) (investible if within 5 years of retirement)
Approx Value _____

☐ 457 (investible if within 5 years of retirement)
Approx Value _____

☐ IRAs (investible) Approx Value_____

If the prospective client has $300K or more in a 401(k), 403(b), 457 or other outside investments, and are within 5 years of retirement, set the appointment.

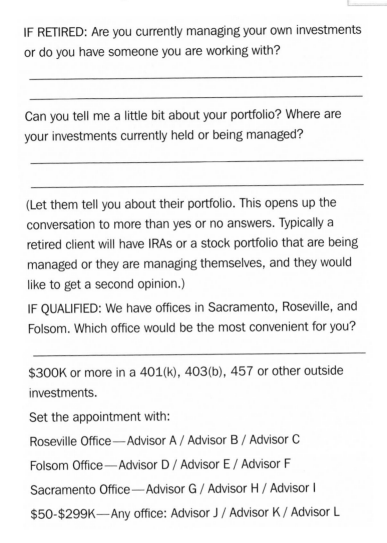

IF RETIRED: Are you currently managing your own investments or do you have someone you are working with?

_____

_____

Can you tell me a little bit about your portfolio? Where are your investments currently held or being managed?

_____

_____

(Let them tell you about their portfolio. This opens up the conversation to more than yes or no answers. Typically a retired client will have IRAs or a stock portfolio that are being managed or they are managing themselves, and they would like to get a second opinion.)

IF QUALIFIED: We have offices in Sacramento, Roseville, and Folsom. Which office would be the most convenient for you?

_____

$300K or more in a 401(k), 403(b), 457 or other outside investments.

Set the appointment with:

Roseville Office—Advisor A / Advisor B / Advisor C

Folsom Office—Advisor D / Advisor E / Advisor F

Sacramento Office—Advisor G / Advisor H / Advisor I

$50-$299K—Any office: Advisor J / Advisor K / Advisor L

A caller who does not meet our account minimum of $50,000 is politely referred to the Financial Planning Association at www.fpanet.org, which provides a database of investment advisors (and their compensation models) available in each region of the country.

After we've vetted a caller's financial situation, we begin the process of collecting *personal* information. We use the following script for every *qualified* caller, as well as callers who will be eligible within five years, who are typically from our niche markets. We then immediately enter the information into our CRM Salesforce database.

We strongly suggest you create similar scripts that support your specific company model.

General Market
First-Time Prospective Client Profile

First Name: _____

Last Name: _____

Greet/Nickname?_____

What is your home mailing address?

_____

City: _____

State: CA   Zip code: _____

Do you have an email address that you use? (We offer a quarterly investment newsletter)

Email Address:_____

@ _____

What is the best contact number to reach you at?

☐ Home: _____

☐ Cell: _____

☐ Work: _____

Are you married or single? _____

Spouse's Name:

First: _____

Last: _____

How did you hear about Hanson McClain? _____

_____

Referred by?_____

Notes: _____

_____

Keywords: _____

☐ IRA   ☐ SEP IRA   ☐ 401(k)   ☐ 457   ☐ 403(b)

☐ Pension w/ lump sum rollover option

☐ Stocks _____

☐ Bonds _____

☐ Mutual Funds _____

☐ Cash _____

No PERS or STRS (retirement plans w/ no lump sum rollover option)

Callers who meet account minimums are offered a complimentary appointment, where their personal financial situation and individual goals are assessed and our fee structure is explained. While we encourage our advisors to pursue commitments from prospective clients, we are a low-pressure firm. We don't sell proprietary products so the initial appointment is as much about us determining whether the client's expectations can be met and whether we feel we can work with *them*, as it is about determining whether *they* feel Hanson McClain Advisors is the best fit for their needs. This is not about being elitist or exclusive. We're a for-profit enterprise. Identifying poor fits for your firm will save you time, hardship, and possibly even a lawsuit down the road. Clients who insist on speaking with you every day cost you money and stress. Eliminating them from consideration *before* they come aboard takes confidence, but maintaining your standards in these circumstances is a part of your success.

If, for *any* reason, we feel someone is not a good fit for our firm, we inform them via letter within three days of the initial appointment.

Campaign Data Collection

The consistent, organized collection of data is intended to reveal, among other things, marketing campaign effectiveness. Therefore, tracking the origin of every caller, along with the cost and the asset capture of each campaign, is crucial. Numbers can then be analyzed in a variety of useful ways, be it to compare specific campaigns, quarter-to-quarter first-time callers, year-to-year marketing spends, and marketing costs per caller, per new client, or per advisor appointment. The possibilities are almost limitless and most have value. Over time, you'll identify assessments that support your specific needs.

A partial list of the types of information we seek through marketing data analyses are:

- Campaign costs
- Number of campaign contacts created
- Campaign assets captured
- Costs, contacts, and assets captured campaign versus campaign
- The cumulative marketing cost for each caller from all campaigns (Yearly total marketing spend, divided by number of callers)
- The marketing cost of each new client per each separate campaign
- Year-to-year comparisons of marketing costs per new clients
- Week-to-week marketing costs per new contacts and new clients
- Quarter-to-quarter marketing costs per new contacts and new clients
- Day-to-day marketing costs compared day-to-day to the previous year

Below is a partial screenshot of our year-to-year broadcast and print campaign summary entry page. This is a master category page depicting the yearly totals (only the first third of 2013 was available), and therefore does not include referrals (33% of new assets in 2012), workshops (17% of new assets in 2012), other types of campaigns, or client acquisition related to community involvement. As an aside, 18% of our new assets in 2012 were placed in the "other" category, which could be attributed to branding.

As you can see, in 2012 we spent $436,689 on broadcast and print advertising for a total accumulation of $28,730,594 in new client assets originating specifically from these campaigns. Interestingly, we spent almost $200,000 more on broadcast and print in 2012 than in 2011, and while this did result in 22 more opportunities — 306 (in 2011) versus 328 (in 2012) — in spite of a significantly *higher spend,* roughly $12,000,000 *fewer* dollars were captured in 2012.

Why?

First, what answers are we seeking? The most obvious question is: Was our overall business down in 2012?

The answer is no. As our referrals, our niche market, and the

Campaign Hierarchy

Campaign Name	Contacts	Opportunities	Won Opportunities
ADV - Parent Campaign (View Parent)	0	0	0
ADV - 2012	328	328	85
ADV - 2011	306	306	107
ADV - 2013	153	153	35
Hierarchy Total	787	787	227

A partial screen capture of the campaign summary entry page. The columns there isn't room to display include Value Won Opportunities (in $), Value Opportunities (in $), Responses, Num Sent, and Actual Cost (in $). ADV is our abbreviation for advertising.

effectiveness of our *other* campaigns actually increased in 2012, it was the best year for growth in Hanson McClain Advisors' company history.

Could the discrepancy be due to an issue with the content of our broadcast and print ad campaigns for 2012?

Probably not, as it wasn't opportunities that were lacking, it was our *closing* ratio, 35% in 2011 (107 new clients out of 306 contacts), versus 26% in 2012 (85 new clients out of 328 contacts), which was down significantly year to year.

This data spurred us to ask the question: Why, in spite of 22 more opportunities, and an almost $200,000 larger spend for print and broadcast campaigns, were the number of opportunities won, along with the actual dollar amounts captured from print and broadcast advertising, lower in 2012, which was an overall banner year?

First, from an internal standpoint, *specifically* in terms of assets captured, after some analysis, a preliminary *partial* answer to this question became evident: 2011 was an outlier. The average amount of investible assets for the new clients captured through print and broadcast was the highest in company history, with a handful of particularly wealthy clients skewing the total of the Value Won Opportunities by several million.

Still, more analysis was required. The *total* number of opportunities had risen but the amount of new clients had fallen.

The answer we were seeking soon became evident. In 2012 we added four new radio stations and one new television station to our advertising rotation. As we have a good grasp of the demographics of the listeners of our local radio stations (and the readers of the local magazines and newspapers), and because we had been saturating the outlets that we *knew* to have *ideal* listening demographics (55–75 years of age) for some years, we had made the calculated decision to experiment with and expand our advertising to stations with a *younger* demographic. This resulted in an increase in calls from younger people with fewer investible assets and no or little experience working with an investment advisor. Many were window shoppers testing the waters who were not ready to commit.

Needless to say, we dropped the new outlets from our rotation at the start of 2013.

On the next page is a *partial* master list of print and broadcast advertising for the years 2011–2013 broken down into a list of individual campaigns. Not all campaigns have been included in this list. Every campaign, from our Northern California radio show to individual static banner ads placed on third-party websites, on down to email blasts and church bulletins, has its own tab and spreadsheets. Simple division can give you cost per contact, etc. At the bottom of the spreadsheet we've included tabs from one of our niche markets.

Behind each tab is a spreadsheet that includes, among other categories, these areas:

- Contacts
- Opportunities won
- Value of new assets won via that specific campaign
- Cost of campaign

Every campaign or other reason that prompts prospective clients to call needs a category and a supporting database (e.g., cost, number of contacts, assets captured, etc.) in your CRM. While it takes just a few moments to set up a category and mere seconds to gather and record this information during the initial contact, the more comprehensive the data, the more synthesized your analysis of the data, and what works and what doesn't work, will be.

Campaign Name
Parent Campaign - ALL
ADV - Parent Campaign
ADV - 2011
ADV - Cap Radio 2011
ADV - Church Bulletins
ADV - Comstock's Magazine 2011
ADV - KFBK/KSTE 2011
ADV - Radio Show 2011
ADV - 2012
ADV - Comstock's Magazine 2012
ADV - KFBK 1530 AM
ADV - KFBK Web Banner Ad
ADV - KHTK 1140 AM
ADV - KNCI 105.1
ADV - KSEG 96.9 FM
ADV - KSTE Talk 650AM
ADV - KXTV News 10
ADV - Radio Show 2012
ADV - Sacramento Magazine
ADV - 2013
ADV - Comstock Mag
ADV - Inside Pubs
ADV - KFBK 2013
ADV - Radio Show 2013
ADV - Sac Mag
REF - MNFA
AT&T - Marketing
DML - Parent Campaign
DML - 2011
DML - Q1 2011 Back on Track
DML - Q1 Email
DML - Q2 2011 Second Opinion
DML - Q2 Email
DML - Q3 2011 Second Opinion
DML - Q4 2011 Nationally Ranked

A partial master list of print and broadcast advertising for the years 2011–2013.

The Sweet Smell of Referrals

Why go the extra mile to keep your existing clients happy when statistics say that they are not all that likely to leave you unless you do a truly poor job?

First, in the electronic age, people have access to more information than ever before. We sometimes get calls from clients who are concerned with obscure financial rumors that may have originated from bogus websites or questionable news sources located in distant countries.

Access to technology also means they are being located and targeted by the competition.

Treating your existing clients well is simply the right thing to do. When it comes to your business, see your clients as your professional spouses and make up your mind that your relationship will forever remain in honeymoon status. Never rest on your laurels and never stop the wooing, because it's a great deal less expensive to keep an existing client than it is to find a new one.

But for the purposes of this section and building your business, one of the main reasons you need to treat your clients well is referrals.

When you're just starting out, marketing and niche marketing are likely going to be the biggest resources for client acquisitions —but also for expenses. It may take a decade before your referrals outpace your marketing in terms of producing new clients and new revenue. Our referrals have made up a larger and larger portion of our new assets every year for the last 15 years. In 2012, referrals were 33% of our new business, not only making it our #1 new client resource, but, with no hard costs, virtually free. This happened *partly* because we never stop marketing to our existing clients.

How do you increase referrals?

■ **Ask.** Make it a point to ask your clients to remember to send their friends your way. You can subtly add this into letters, emails, and most importantly, by mentioning it whenever you see a client. Remember, whether it's a doctor, attorney, dentist, or an investment advisor, just about everyone likes the feeling that comes with believing they had the foresight to pick the best anything available. Ask for referrals, and ye shall receive.

■ **Acknowledgment.** When you get a referral, make sure you send the referrer a gift or thank-you card. On their birthdays, send flowers or a gift card.

■ **Never stop marketing to your existing clients.** Newsletters, press releases, letters, and touches "just because." These, combined with exemplary service, should build your business. If you are doing things the right way, in time your existing clients will bring you more business than any single category of marketing.

Below is one of our favorite lists: Referrals for the past year. With Value Won Opportunities as high as almost 60% (and just because a referral hasn't come aboard *yet* doesn't mean they won't), it obviously helps to have great word of mouth.

Campaign Hierarchy		
Campaign Name	Value Won Opportunities	Value Opportunities
REF - Parent Campaign (View Parent)	$0	$0
FIRM Generated	$24,265,152	$49,926,678
REF - Client	$52,651,730	$91,703,527
REF - Future Client	$3,738,792	$11,142,793
REF - Professional Resource	$9,844,493	$22,622,126
Word of Mouth	$17,611,120	$59,623,256
REF - TDA RSVL	$0	$2,000,000
REF - TDA NATIONAL PACIFIC	$0	$0
Hierarchy Total	$108,111,287	$237,018,380

The value of referrals.

The Actual Cost of a Direct Mailer

Some advisors and marketers believe that direct mailers are old-fashioned and not worth the cost. We disagree. Below is an expanded campaign result from a *single* mailer from 2012, sent by us through a third-party originator (we write the letter, they do the rest) to 34,505 recipients in the 55- to 75-years-old demographic. The recipients are spread out over the three most populous counties in the Sacramento region. From this mailer came 45 opportunities, of which we won 10. While 22% is not an outstanding number, there *are* a few numbers here that are very satisfying.

First, the entire hard cost of the mailer was $24,175, meaning

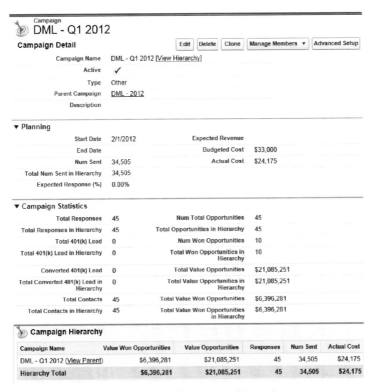

The results of one DML (direct mail letter) campaign.

it cost $537 for each response, while it cost $2,417 for each new client. (There are 10 new clients at this time, but more of the 45 opportunities may come aboard). Best of all, the $6,396,281 in new assets represents an average of $639,000 per new client. That's a good number, and it means that the bottom line of this *one simple campaign* should result in over $64,000 in revenue in the first year alone.

Weekly Analysis That Drives Decision Making

Earlier we mentioned that we had recently raised our HMA account minimum from $250,000 to $300,000, and had, in 2010, created a new account category called "Select," which is reserved for clients with investible assets starting at $50,000 and topping out at $300,000. The graph below is one of the resources that motivated the change.

Each week, the marketing department documents the number of *both* qualified and non-qualified new callers. On Fridays, the information is pasted into the body of an email and sent to each advisor. Simple. Clean. Fast.

But that's not the end of it. Before the creation of our Select division, we realized that we were referring as many as 20 callers a week to the www.fpanet.org website where, in theory, they would choose a competitor. Further analysis showed that many of these potential clients fell just short of our then account minimum of $250,000.

Week #20	New Contacts	New Appts
2013 / 2012	24 / 11	
HMA	14	10
Cost per HMA Appt		$800
Select	10	5
AT&T	0	0
Non Qualified Calls	2	
• $25K CD/IRA		
• $0		

A statistical breakdown of contacts we received during the 28th week of June 2013.

Below is a comparison of new callers (without regard for the resource, which is tabulated elsewhere) for the 28th week of both 2013 and 2012. Of the 24 calls received in 2013, if our policy had not changed, 10 would have been referred to www.fpanet.org and perhaps found an advisor there. Even predicting a 20% close ratio, in one year that's still 204 clients we would have turned away.

Too many.

It was the repetition of this data that prompted us to create a business model that would both provide for these clients *and* be profitable for Hanson McClain Advisors.

In the 28th week of 2013, we scheduled five new appointments for the Select division that, if successful, will result in *a minimum* of $250,000 in additional assets under advisement for our firm.

Overall, from the 24 first-time callers from the 28th week of 2013, we've scheduled 15 new appointments, 10 of which are for HMA (upwards of $300,000 in investible assets). As we spend roughly $8,000 a week on print and broadcast marketing, this amounts to $800 spent per HMA new client appointment. (We don't include the Select division in our marketing spend calculations.)

This one simple chart, reconstituted weekly for several years, often showed (in the Non-Qualified Calls category) possible clients with $100,000 to even $200,000 in investible assets being turned away.

Just three years in, and our Select division has almost $90 million under management.

Quarterly Newsletter Requests

We've presented a cross section of the types of data we use to, among other things, identify the success of our campaigns, the value of referrals, and even a week-to-week general overview for "at a glance" purposes. But what about our ongoing marketing unrelated to more traditional advertising? We write and distribute a quarterly investment newsletter that goes out to over

7,000 people (1,200 hard copies and 6,000 electronic copies). Our newsletter has nine lives and hard copies can show up in some unexpected locations (e.g., doctor's offices, barbershops, pinned to the board in golf course clubhouses, etc.). Our newsletter is a "touch" that commands tracking and analyzing. It is unique in that it is a marketing piece intended for both current *and prospective* clients. As a sidelight, requests by non-clients for our newsletter have steadily increased over time.

We promote our newsletter on our radio program, on our banner ads, and in various other marketing pieces. We also display copies on a magazine stand in the lobbies of our offices. We've come to understand that a newsletter is an unintimidating resource for potential clients to become acquainted with our firm. Because of this, we decided it might be useful to track the origin of new requests for copies. We wanted to know where the people who request our newsletter found out about it.

The graph on the next page is automatically generated from a spreadsheet to help us visualize the origins of first time newsletter requests.

Marketing and Budgets

While we spent just over $1 million on marketing in 2012, this contributed to more than $200 million in new assets to manage for Hanson McClain Advisors. So even the immediate, first-year return on our marketing investment represented a substantial net gain.

We understand that implementing every campaign we've touched on in this book isn't going to be feasible for everyone, as there was a time when we couldn't afford a graphic designer to create our logo.

While we are careful to monitor our expenses and to make corrections when our data shows we have invested in a flawed or failed campaign, we are extremely aggressive about utilizing as much free or soft-cost marketing at possible.

We utilize technology to "touch" inactive prospective clients with email correspondence, including letters and newsletters, company announcements and press releases. We call this "dripping on inactive clients," and it's a marketing approach with almost no associated costs.

Just as surely as you never stop marketing to your *existing* clients, inactive clients need attention as well. You've already invested the hard marketing costs that spurred them to call your firm and perhaps even had them in for an appointment or two, so don't let those hard costs go to waste: Keep after them. Send them all possible electronic communications.

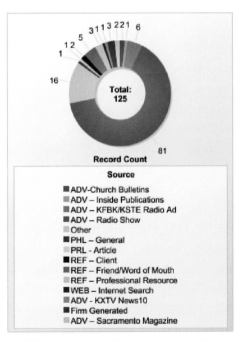

The origins of first-time newsletter requests during a specific period.

Other Budget Analytics Tools

Let's say you want to implement numerous marketing campaigns next quarter. The problem is that your office only consists of you, another advisor, and an assistant. (And your CRM is a legal pad, a computer, and an Excel spreadsheet.)

Just in case there is any doubt, let us repeat: Compiling statistics and information on your marketing campaigns is hugely important.

Here's something we've done that meets any budget and can be both effective and efficient: renting different phone lines for every campaign. Companies such as Ifbyphone.com are voice-based marketing automation firms. Most of the plans are under $100, and you get to select your phone numbers. Say you have ten campaigns going on at once, which is not impossible or expensive if you utilize electronic newsletters, email blasts, marketing letters, social media, banner ads, and so on. Each time someone calls a particular number that was printed directly on a mailer or in an email blast, as you answer the phone a "whisper message" that only you can hear tells you the source of the call. (All the calls are funneled into your main phone number.) The beauty of this (for those firms without sophisticated client management software) is that Ifbyphone.com *automatically* creates detailed reports that you can print out and analyze.

Results You Don't Immediately See

The overall or long-term effectiveness of a campaign may not be immediately apparent. That's not to say you should stay with a campaign that isn't working; it's simply a reminder that even modestly successful campaigns may continue to pay off a number of ways over time. First, for every campaign spreadsheet showing the acquisition of 10 new clients out of, say, 50 new contacts created, over time it's likely that *some* of the 40 who got away will in fact eventually come aboard. You increase the odds of this happening by continuing to "drip" on them with electronic marketing correspondence.

Second, today's marketing campaigns help to build your brand both now and in the future. Every campaign makes an impression that lasts well beyond the length of the advertisement or the life of the page in the magazine.

Document and store data from every campaign. This means that the first question you should ask *every first-time caller* is "How did you hear about us?"

In Closing

As we prepared to write this book, we naturally looked at the work of academics and other advisors in the field of marketing. There are any number of books available on this topic, but the lessons therein are often simplistic, short on specifics, or entirely theory-driven.

What you've just read is the composition that resulted from the realization that just about every other book we've read was holding back the very materials the readers — advisors looking to grow their businesses — actually needed. We realized that if we wanted to write a book with usable *and original* content, the only way to do so was to present our entire marketing approach. This is what we at Hanson McClain Advisors have done to grow our firm to almost $1.6 billion in assets under management in 20 years. Any omissions are due to space constraints or simple oversight.

We sincerely hope you are able to utilize every bit of information presented here in *Investment Advisor Marketing: A Pathway to Growing Your Firm and Building Your Brand* to great effect.

Best of luck to you!

Scott Hanson & Pat McClain

For interviews, to arrange for Scott Hanson or Pat McClain to speak at your company or private event, to order quarterly newsletters, or to learn more about Pathway Strategic Advisors or Hanson McClain Advisors, please contact:

Pathway Strategic Advisors
110 Woodmere Rd. Suite 250
Folsom, CA 95630
www.pathwaysa.com
877-697-2849

Hanson McClain Advisors
8775 Folsom Blvd Suite 100
Sacramento, CA 95826
www.hansonmcclain.com
888-979-4077

For additional information about
Investment Advisor Marketing:
A Pathway to Growing Your Firm and Building Your Brand,
email queries to info@irishcanonpress.com.

Investment Advisor Marketing:
is available in all e-formats, and wherever books are sold.

For bulk discounts, or media-copy review requests, please contact info@irishcanonpress.com.

To listen to Scott and Pat's weekly radio program, Money Matters, tune in Saturdays from 10:00 to 11:00 a.m. PST to 1530 KFBK AM Sacramento (also rebroadcast Sundays from 2:00 to 3:00 p.m.), at www.kfbk.com, or via podcast, 24/7, at www.moneymatters.com.

Scott Hanson, Pat McClain, and Pathway Strategic Advisors are on LinkedIn.

Follow Hanson McClain Advisors on Facebook:
https://www.facebook.com/HansonMcClain

Sean Harvey can be reached at
sean.harvey@hansonmcclain.com